PLANNING CITIES 101
A PRACTICAL INTRODUCTION

by
Marilyn and Carl Stephani

© Copyright 2017
All Rights Reserved
No part of this book may be used or reproduced in any manner whatsoever without written permission, except in the case of brief quotations embodied in critical articles and reviews. For information contact the authors at: carl@carlstephani.com

Carl and Marilyn Stephani
5505 East 110th Place
Tulsa, Oklahoma 74137

ISBN-13:978-1544848808
ISBN-10: 1544848803

TABLE OF CONTENTS

PREFACE. 1

INTRODUCTION. 3

TERMINOLOGY. 5
    CITY OR MUNICIPALITY. 5
    CITY PLANS. 5
    LAND "DEVELOPMENT". 5
    PLANNING, ZONING AND SUBDIVIDING. 6
    POLICY. 8

PART I - THE STRUCTURE AND CONTENT OF CITY PLANS. 9

STRUCTURE - THE ELEMENTS. 11
    LAND USE. 12
    TRANSPORTATION. 14
    CONSERVATION. 16
    OTHER ELEMENTS. 17

CONTENTS - THE PRESCRIPTIONS. 19
    GOALS. 20
    OBJECTIVES. 21
    POLICIES. 22
    PROGRAMS. 23
    ACTIVITIES. 24
    ACTIONS. 25
    SUMMARY. 26

PART II - PREPARING A CITY PLAN. 27

WHAT NEEDS TO DONE?. 29

WHY DO IT?. 34
    IDEALISM/UTOPIANISM. 34
    ISSUE PROMOTION. 34
    NEIGHBORHOOD ENHANCEMENT. 34
    POPULARITY. 35
    STATE OR FEDERAL MANDATES. 35

INITIATING THE PLAN PREPARATION PROCESS. 36
    MOTIVATION. 36
    STAFFING. 37
        Councils of Government & Regional Planning
            Organizations. 42
        Educational Institution and Others. 42

PART III - THE CITIZENS' ADVISORY COMMITTEE. 45

COMMITTEE PROTOCOL. 46

COMMITTEE STRUCTURE. 46
    BYLAWS TEMPLATE WITH COMMENTARY.. 47
    BYLAWS TEMPLATE MODEL. 55

COMMITTEE STARTUP. 57
    LETTER OF INVITATION TO THE MEMBERS.. 57
    AGENDA TEMPLATE FOR THE FIRST MEETING. 58

PART IV - THE SUBSTANCE OF PLANNING.. 61

PART V - THE LAW. 65
    OVERVIEW. 66
    INTERPRETATION OF STATE STATUTES. 67
    OTHER CONSIDERATIONS. 71

APPENDICES.. 73

PREFACE

City plans in the United States today are frequently lengthy complex documents that are difficult to read, interpret, and implement. This book is an attempt to address that problem. City plans should be accessible and useable by the average citizen, and they can be if their contents are properly analyzed and screened for actual planning content.

In this book we have attempted to give you a handbook for understanding your city's general plan in a way that few are able to master. PART I of this book describes conceptually the structure and content of city plans - usually several "Elements" each including a list of policy statements. PART II describes why plans are prepared and explains one way to go about preparing one. PART III presents the organizational structure for a citizens' advisory committee to advise on the preparation of a plan. With these tools newly elected public officials should be able to properly oversee the preparation of a plan for their city; to assure that it contains what it must, and not more than it should; and to establish a viable citizens' advisory committee to help get the job done right.

An over-riding concept that is emphasized throughout this book is the assertion that many plans currently "on the books" are bloated because their authors have mixed the directive language of planning with the descriptive language of information. City plans inevitably will contain two types of language: (1) Descriptive statements that tell you about the facts; and (2) policy language that sets direction.

To declare that the population in a given city has increased by some percentage over the past decade is to make a descriptive statement.

To state that the population growth in a given city should not be permitted to increase by more than some percentage over the next decade is a prescriptive statement.

A proper city "plan" is a prescription. It is a guide for decision-making to lead the city from its current condition to a more healthy future; just as a medical prescription is a tool for leading a person from their current state to a more healthy future.

The language contained in a city plan (like a medical prescription), is based in many cases, on voluminous information and analyses. Nevertheless, when the doctor issues the prescription, it is not issued with copies of all the information that has been gathered about the patient and the analyses of that information. The prescription is issued as a simple statement with the name of the appropriate pharmaceutical.

In the case of the city plan, however, all too often the prescription is issued along with, or buried someplace within, all the information that a city planner has gathered about the city, including the analyses of that information. That makes many city plans very difficult for the average citizen if they wish to use the plan to support or oppose some planning related activity, or action, taking place in their community.

This book is intended to remedy that problem by making the structure, organization, and content of city plans more apparent so that those who user their city plans will understand how to quickly get to the parts of a plan relevant to their needs. It also provides a guide to writing a new user-friendly city plan.

INTRODUCTION

City plans are basically very simple documents. They comprise chapters which are called "Elements", which are each dedicated to a topic area, for instance, land use, transportation, environment, etcetera. Then within each element there is language that gives direction to decision-making - prescriptive language. This language is usually referred to in a weak hierarchical order as "goals," "objectives," "policies," "programs," "activities," and "actions."

Google defines a "plan" as "a detailed proposal for doing or achieving something." Thus, the Goals, Objectives, Policies, Programs, Activities, and Actions in your city's plan comprise THE PLAN. They are detailed proposals for doing or achieving. Everything else contained in the document called "the plan" is descriptive information - the collection of facts upon which the prescription, which is the PLAN, is based. It would be much easier for the general public if most of the descriptive information in a city plan would be included in a separate document given a different name, such as, "City Plan Environmental Scan," or "City Plan Background Information Report," or "City Plan Supplemental Information," etcetera, but that is often not the case.

Unfortunately for the non-professional user, what often happens is that planners prepare the prescriptive language for their plans and then pile a huge amount of descriptive material on top of it, making the search for the prescriptions much more difficult than it needs to be, or should be. There are exceptions.

Planning is an important role of government and it becomes more important daily as the population of the world increasingly continues to urbanize. Planning helps us keep out of each others' way, just as common table manners help us enjoy meals together. The vacuum created by the ignorance, or lack of planning will often be filled by conflict and resolved in violence. Planning is the peaceful alternative to social chaos and the hope of democracy for the stability it needs to thrive. We need good planning and this book is intended to help us achieve it.

This book is also intended as a companion to ZONING 101: A PRACTICAL INTRODUCTION, which was originally published by the National League of Cities, and which is still available thru www.amazon.com. Zoning is a tool that can be used to help bring about the results envisioned by a plan, as is a capital improvement program, a subdivision ordinance (or development code), and a budget.

Finally, this book is also intended to help officials in smaller jurisdictions understand in practical terms how to determine how much they actually need to do (which means "to spend") to meet the planning requirements that other levels of government might impose upon them, as well as what they might choose to do beyond that. Although its primary audience might be smaller cities and towns, many municipal officials and civic-minded citizens from larger jurisdictions could also learn from its contents.

Planning for an entire city may seem like an overwhelming task, but it doesn't have to be. Cities have been planned, one way or another, since they were first "invented"; and, before that, groups of people who found themselves settling new areas doubtless discussed where they were going build their houses or set up their tents, where they were going to have their latrines, etcetera. That was the city planning for that day.

Planning is carried on at many levels. When you moved into an apartment or a house, you probably planned which rooms you were going to use for what purposes, which cabinets would be for clothing, for food, for pots and pans, etcetera. That's planning.

We all plan all the time in anticipation of events or future outcomes, like the planting of a garden.

City planning is different in scale, but not in concept, from all this other planning that we do. The most significant difference between the planning we do as individuals and the planning that is done by a city is that city plans often have requirements set for them in the laws of the state, and, in some cases, in federal grant programs for which the city wishes to qualify. In addition, some states have state and regional plans with which city plans must be consistent, and some federal programs have requirements for certain types of city planning.

TERMINOLOGY

There is a terminology associated with this book, and with city planning in general, that can tend to make planning related discussions become unnecessarily obscure to the novice. Following are several terms with explanations of their usage in this book and in the planning profession which should prove helpful to anyone seeking to become involved in the planning discussion.

CITY OR MUNICIPALITY

For the purposes of this book a "municipality" refers to a city, county, town, township, borough, village, or other multi-purpose local government similar to any of these. For convenience, this book refers to all of these interchangeably as "cities," "municipalities," "towns," or "jurisdictions," and refers to the governing bodies of municipalities generically as "city councils".

CITY PLANS

Across the country, city plans are variously referred to as General Plans, Master Plans, Comprehensive Plans, Plans of Conservation and Development, etc., etc., and etcetera. There is no consistency nationwide among those who write the laws relating to such plans in the usage of these terms. It's like "garage" sales and "tag" sales. In different parts of the country, different terms are used to refer to the same thing. In this book we refer to all of them generically as "city plans."

LAND "DEVELOPMENT"

When used by planners this term refers to things that are done with, or on, the land. For example, Land can be "developed" for sand and gravel extraction, or for construction of a residential neighborhood. Either use would change the land from its natural state to some other condition. When that occurs the land is referred to as "developed", even though it may just be developed as a Christmas tree farm and it may look very much like the forest that surrounds it.

PLANNING, ZONING AND SUBDIVIDING

Ultimately city planning relates to the zoning of land, and the buying and selling of pieces of land, generally referred to as "parcels," or "lots," which is real property that people own.

The division of land for sale, generally speaking, is controlled by a city's subdivision ordinance.

If you own some land which you want to divide into several pieces, you will need to learn something about your city's subdivision ordinance. That ordinance will tell you what the relationship must be between the width and depth of each piece ("lot") which you are allowed to create. It may also tell you how much street frontage each lot you create must have and what procedures you will have to follow to create the pieces so that you can legally sell them. It may also include other restrictions on how you can divide your property as it relates to water bodies, hillsides or other geographic features, "panhandle" shapes, etcetera.

Many cities have separate ordinances - "Lot Split" ordinances - that regulate the division of one piece of land into two pieces. Lot Split Ordinances are usually much less restrictive than subdivision ordinances. Subdivision ordinances generally regulate the division of land into three or more pieces.

There is an interesting terminological anomaly here in that "lots" are not created through the Lot Split Ordinance:
- If you create two pieces of land out of one piece following the requirements of the "lot split" ordinance, you are creating two "parcels."
- If you create three or more pieces of land out of one piece following the requirements of the subdivision ordinance, your are creating "lots."

Parcels are identified by their aliquot description, or by a "metes and bounds" description. An aliquot description is based on the system of townships, ranges, and sections into which most of the United States is divided for survey purposes. A metes and bounds description is based on survey landmarks.

"Lots" are identified by the number that they are assigned in the subdivision within which they exist, which must be given a name, such as "Rolling Hills Estates." That is one of the great conveniences that subdividing land, as opposed to splitting land, provides. Identifying property in a subdivision is much easier than understanding a metes and bounds or aliquot description of a parcel created by a lot split.

For a convenient more detailed description of how lots and parcels came to be, see THE LAND SYSTEM OF THE UNITED STATES: An Introduction to the History and Practice of Land Use and Land Tenure, by Marion Clawson published in 1968.

Zoning ordinances are related to subdivision ordinances in that they prescribe the minimum size of any lot or parcel that is proposed to be separated from a larger piece of property. Zoning ordinances also prescribe what land can be used for. For more on that subject see ZONING 101: A Practical Introduction, Third Edition.

Zoning and subdivision ordinances are "ordinances," which means they are laws. City Plans, on the other hand, may be adopted as ordinances, or they may be adopted as something lesser, as policies. Policies differ from ordinances in that a violation of a law can be punished by fines and/or imprisonment; whereas violations of policies are not. For example, a city might adopt an ordinance that prohibits retail establishments from its residential areas. Violations of such a law would have punishments associated with it. On the other hand, a city may adopt a policy that states that it encourages its residents to purchase only low emission vehicles. There would be no punishment associated with a violation of a policy.

Zoning and subdivision ordinances, and virtually all general plans are adopted by the city council after at least one public hearing, and, in most cases an additional prior public hearing by a planning commission.

During the last century city plans generally began being written as city policies intended to guide decisions to a desired future condition; such as a policy to discourage billboards within the city limits. In many states these plans continue as general guides. In a good number of states, however, city plans have evolved into the status of ordinances such that subdivision and zoning ordinances must be written to strictly abide by the statements of policy contained in the plans.

Originally, city plans were visionary documents, intended to describe the image of the city toward which individual day-to-day actions were to be guided, but not specifically prescribed. Over the past forty years in many cities and states there has been a tendency to change these plans so that they are no longer simply advisory guides for decision-making but have become strictly regulatory and strictly enforced.

It is important to know in every city how regulatory city and state laws allow their plans to be. In some cities, portions of city plans are regulatory, but other portions are not. In other cities, the entire city plans are considered regulatory and enforceable; and in yet other cities, their city plans are considered strictly advisory. The plans of many cities are in transition from generally advisable policy guides, to strictly enforced prescriptions. The more enforceable they are, the more important it is to understand them and how they are created. That is what this book is intended to help you do.

POLICY

The term "policy" can be confusing in that it can refer generally to any statement (goal, objective, program, activity, or action) that indicates support or opposition to something; and, it can also refer to any specific statement which indicates support or opposition to some action *which is not a goal, objective, program, activity or action.* In that sense, it can be compared to the term "Kleenex," which can refer to a specific brand of paper product; or can also be used to refer to all similar paper products regardless of brand.

PART I - THE STRUCTURE AND CONTENT OF CITY PLANS

STRUCTURE - THE ELEMENTS

To understand what city planning is in our day it may be useful to go back in time. The Romans had plans to guide those who established new Roman settlements thousands of years ago.

Going beyond that, let's conceptually visit some of the first city planners.

They lived with their family, or a small group of people someplace where they felt relatively comfortable and safe. They prospered and realized that their group was getting bigger each year as babies were born, and visitors decided to stay and became residents.

Some of them realized that if their homes and businesses continued to grow helter-skelter, then one day their settlement might be so completely built up for quite a distance that they would have no central place for special events or other public gatherings.

LAND USE

So, they went to their city council, or group leaders, whoever they were, and told them:

> "Instead of allowing people to just keep building their houses wherever they wish, the city council should designate some open land someplace in the central part of the city that would be kept free of buildings so that it could be used by the town's people for a gathering place."

That very well could have been the start of what we call "land use planning." By definition we don't have any written record about those times, but from the plans we have of ancient cities, there is evidence that many of them had such places, and such places would not likely have resulted fortuitously; i.e., they must have been planned. Thus, land use planning for a city - "city planning" - began, and the first "element" of a city plan was the "Land Use Element" - which is intended to answer the question: how are we going to allow land to be used in our city?

Since that time the practice of city planning has gotten into more depth, and has been refined. Even today city plans which might only contain land use elements are generally refined enough to deal with different types of primary land uses: Residential, commercial, industrial, and often agricultural uses.

Then even the most simple plans often have amplified descriptions of their proposed residential areas such that they designate areas for high density residential development, medium density, low density, and other residential densities ad infinitum. Similarly with commercial, industrial and agricultural uses. In addition to those refinements, many city plans identify areas for open space uses, historic uses, or other uses - for example "river-related uses" - which deal with the specific characteristics of their particular natural and cultural environments.

The term "land use" should not be feared or mystified. It simply refers to how land is used - for example, growing trees. Horticulture, is a land use; so is growing tomatoes, or selling cars, or excavating rock, or selling clothing. Each of these is a way of using either the substance of the land itself or the surface of the land. "Land use" is one of the foundations of city planning. Virtually everything that has to do with planning has its roots in land use and the regulation and control of the use of land.

There is often a multitude of different land uses on the maps of modern city plans, and those uses change over time as those plans are amended. And they are justly amended from time to time as land uses change. For example, in the 1980s, video rental stores were the craze. Today we no longer see video rental stores at all. Such services as blacksmith shops and urban stables have also largely departed the scene.

City plans do not attempt to identify every single type of land use. Instead, city plans generally group land uses in relation to their recommendations about where different land uses should, or should not be allowed.

There is no single nationwide standard for categorizing land uses as there is, for instance, for traffic signs. Often city plans rely upon common usage to define the uses that fall under any particular plan policy. There are, however, systems of land use classification that some plans utilize to help categorize their land uses, including the Land Based Classification Standards (LBCS) of the American Planning Association, the Florida land use, cover and forms classification system, and others in use across the country.

The purpose of land use classification systems is to allow planners, engineers, and others involved in land use identification and regulation to refer to groups of land uses without having to use exhaustive lists. Many smaller jurisdictions just rely on common usage names for their land use groupings.

TRANSPORTATION

With the concept of land use planning in mind, it would have been easy for the other elements of city planning to have been conceived.

> "If we are going to set aside a central area, or maybe a number of areas, where we can get together for special events, maybe we should also designate some special roadways that lead to these areas so that they could be made larger than our other roadways, and so that we could get to our special events, and back home again, without stepping on each other."

So they designated several roads to be wider than the rest and those eventually were called "arterials." The smaller streets were called "collectors" because they collected traffic from the neighborhoods. Then the smallest streets, which led to individual residences, were called "local" streets.

> Just as there are classification systems for categorizing land uses, there are classification systems for roadways. The most common is the Functional Classification System of the US Department of Transportation, which refers to roads in relation to their function. Thus if you want to have a certain policy apply to streets that are used to provide access to individual homes, you don't need to name each street individually in a city plan, you simply refer to "residential," or "local," streets and the policy will apply to all streets that function as residential streets. An example would be: "All residential streets should have landscaped verges along their curbs." Streets can also be classified by the volume of traffic are designed for, or the limitations that are on them for access to them.

The designation of some roads as locals, collectors, and arterials is the nucleus of a transportation planning element. This element is expanded in many city plans to deal with trains, ships, aircraft, pipelines, off-road vehicles, bicyclists, pedestrians, equestrians, and others.

With their land use and transportation "elements" in place, and the thought processes that gave rise to them engaged, it would not have been hard for other planning elements to have been conceived.

CONSERVATION

Returning to our pre-history group of planners, they may have also had thoughts about the conservation of their environment.

> "When we cut the trees along the river, the river cuts into the bank which may cause it someday to flood our settlement. Let's not cut down trees along the banks of the river so that these trees can help stabilize the river banks for us."

Thus was born the nucleus of their conservation element.

In today's jargon such a statement as the one quoted above would be called a "conservation policy." Along with related goals, objectives, programs, and activities, this policy would be grouped in a section of a plan called the "Conservation Element" of the city plan. In concept, every "Element" of a city plan should at the very least have a goal; just as every automobile should have a driver's seat. Beyond that, each element of a plan may, or may not, have an objective, or objectives, policies, programs and activities or actions. Examples of these can easily be found in any existing city plan.

OTHER ELEMENTS

Some city plans only have a few elements; others have a dozen or more depending upon how detailed the city wishes to get in specifying the policies they wish to express.

For instance, some plans contain a Housing Element which might include statements about where and how different income-level housing should be integrated into new developments. Other plans include Public Facilities Elements, which might show where new schools, fire or police stations, libraries, parks, churches, sporting and performance venues, and other public facilities could be located; or Public Utilities Elements which might show the locations of future high voltage power transmission lines, water and wastewater collection and treatment facilities, and other similar facilities. The number of "Elements" in a Plan depends upon the desires of the city, as well as the state and federal requirements the Plan is intended to meet.

Sometimes cities choose not to include sets of policies related to a particular topic, for example economic development, as an element of their city plan but prefer to have a separate stand-alone plan for those policies. They might do that to provide more individual emphasis to those policies, or to avoid having them fall under the requirements for content and adoption that the state law would require their city plan to meet.

CONTENTS - THE PRESCRIPTIONS

Switching back now to the theoretical pre-history group that introduced us in the last chapter to the concept of the "elements" of a city plan, as that group began to think about their settlement, they may have realized that in addition to grouping their thoughts about the future of their city into several different topical elements, within each element, as they thought together about their city, they realized that the thoughts they had could also be differentiated in relation to the time table for their accomplishment.

GOALS

For example, after making initial decisions about how to lay out their settlement, they may have decided to project their thinking forward in anticipation of future growth. Instead of just designating certain roadways for arterial status (in other words, larger roads to handle heavier traffic), they might have agreed upon a statement about their transportation network and how they wanted it to serve them.

> "Let's have a transportation system that not only serves those of us who are walking, but also serves those who travel on horseback, bicycle, or chariot, and which seeks to provide safety as well as convenient access." (GOAL)

That statement would then begin to be used to evaluate future decision-making about how the system would be developed. In modern planning language, a statement like the one quoted above would be called a goal:

> A "Goal" is: A statement about a future state or condition that the city would like to achieve and against which current actions can be evaluated.

The core of any city plan is its goals. They describe in conceptual terms the direction in which the city would like its specific actions each day to take. A goal for an individual might be: "To become more physically fit." There is no final arrival point; you can never ultimately reach "more physically fit," but you can consider all your actions in relation to whether they move you in the direction of becoming more physically fit or not. That's what goals do - they give you a direction, not a destination.

OBJECTIVES

Then, as they thought further about their transportation system and its safety and convenience, someone brought up the subject of sidewalks.

Some of their streets had landscape strips between the curbs and sidewalks, and others had sidewalks right up against the curbs. They had more accidents where the sidewalks were right up against the curbs. If one of their goals was to have a transportation network that provides safety for both vehicles and pedestrians, then they should have landscape strips (verges) between all the curbs and the sidewalks.

> "Lets seek to create grass strips along 10% of the roads that do not have them each year, so that in 10 years all our roads will be that way." (OBJECTIVE)

This is an objective because it creates a specific yardstick against which actions can be measured over time. Objectives are the second most important statements included in a city plan. They give the city a way to measure how well it is achieving its goals. They must be measurable to be a proper objective.

POLICIES

Then a question arises in relation to new streets.

> "Let's require that anyone who builds a new street must include in the design of that street a system of curbs that all have grass strips (road verges) along them." (POLICY)

This is a policy statement. It also serves to achieve a goal, but not in a given time period, as an objective would. It is a commitment to act in a certain way to achieve a goal whenever a certain situation arises; in this case, whenever a new road is built, but, unless the plan with this policy has been adopted as an ordinance, the policy is not strictly enforceable. To make it more enforceable it could be adopted as a stand-alone ordinance, or as a part of a subdivision, or even, a zoning ordinance.

PROGRAMS

Then, to enhance the appearance of these road verges,

> "Let's encourage people to plant trees in the verges by offering free striplings to those who would like to do such plantings." (PROGRAM)

This statement relates to a PROGRAM, which is another action than relates to the goal of having a safe and convenient community transportation network. Some city plans contain proposals for many programs, others may contain none.

Programs may be funded by grants, municipal general funds, a dedicated tax, or other means.

ACTIVITIES

Then, to encourage the proper maintenance of these verges,

> "Let's have an annual recognition picnic for those who have most creatively or beautifully planted and maintained verges in front of their properties."
> (ACTIVITY)

This statement relates to an ACTIVITY, which is another action related to the over-arching transportation goal. Like programs, some plans contain proposals for many activities; others may contain none.

ACTIONS

Finally,

> "Let's identify the sidewalks along properties that are owned by the city and create landscaped verges along each of them just as we are requiring our citizens to do." (ACTION)

SUMMARY

If nothing more were done, this meager list including a Goal, an Objective, a Policy, a Program and an Activity could serve as the embryo for a full-fledged city plan transportation element; and could even serve as a full-fledged plan, depending upon the city and how much it wanted to cover in its city plan.

The substance of a plan element comprises statements of policy including goals, objectives, policies, programs, and actions or activities. Not every element needs to have all of these types of policy statements, but to be a plan element there needs to be at least one policy in it. Here is an example of some possible policy statements of each type as related to a theoretical transportation element:

- Goal - Improve transportation safety in the city
- Objective - Reduce the annual number of serious traffic accidents per capita in the city by 10% over the next five years
- Policy - Support the installation of traffic calming features when a majority of the residents in a neighborhood request them
- Programs - participate in the annual statewide traffic safety awareness week events, and other related events
- Activities, or actions - Install traffic calming "humps" in the streets bordering the city hall property.

There is no limit to the number of such statements you can have in your plan, although to be conceptually correct, every objective, policy, program, activity or action should be subsumed under an overarching goal. Some plans choose to not be conceptually correct and include, for instance, an objective or two for which there is no over-arching goal. That is a choice that can be made similar to giving a gift without wrapping it in gift-wrap.

PART II - PREPARING A CITY PLAN

WHAT NEEDS TO DONE?

A city plan is a statement, or series of statements, usually including maps, about how you would like to see something look, operate, or be in the future. If your city wants to prepare a city plan, or is required to prepare a plan in order to satisfy a state or federal requirement, and you are involved in the decision-making process about what the plan will contain, the first thing you should do is to obtain a copy of the document that requires your city to prepare a plan. If there is such a document, then you need to get a copy of it so that you know what is going to be expected of you. If there is no such document, then you are free to include in your plan as much, or as little, as you think necessary.

In many states the guiding document would be a copy of the state statues regarding long-range planning. Do not be daunted by the state statutes. Your city attorney, your state municipal league, state representative, senator, or League of Women Voters should all be able to help you find a copy of the state statutes on planning, if there are any in your state. If there are none, then your city is free to prepare whatever it wants in the way of a city plan within the constraints of the State and Federal Constitutions. If there are planning statutes in your state, they will probably be a dozen or so pages in length, and, if you ignore all the references and footnotes, the substance of the planning statutes is usually written at the 8th grade level and very easy to understand. Planning is a craft, not a science.

You should read the statutes on planning as well as the statutes on state or regional planning, if there are any. Knowledge is power, and, if you want to have the power to have an impact on your plan, you should read the statutes. Your knowledge of the statutes will be invaluable to you as you relate to attorneys, citizens, consultants, planners, and politicians regarding your city plan and your city's planning processes.

Be reminded when you read the statutes that the "law" is written by the legislature, but decisions of judges, "case law," can modify what you read in the statutes. Just having read the statutes does not make you an expert on your state's law on planning, but it gives you a good foundation. Case law is what attorneys research for you when you need the latest interpretation of what the current law is on any particular issue.

When someone used to talk about a "city plan" they used to be referring to planning about how land is to be allowed to be used. Over the years, however, it has become obvious that transportation facilities are intimately related to how land is used. For example, if you allow development of a shopping center in a certain location, you must also prepare to handle the traffic it will create; and, if you construct an intersection of two four-lane divided roadways, you will probable create demand for commercial uses in the area of that intersection. Thus, these days, when someone talks about "city planning," they are usually referring to plans with at least land use and transportation elements.

Many cities engage in a formal city planning process because they have a history of planning covering decades, or even centuries. Some cities, such as Washington, D.C., were planned from their very beginnings; others have only taken up the practice more recently; and some have yet to complete their first formal city plan.

Regardless of the depth of their experience in planning, virtually all cities and towns may find themselves required at some time by the laws of their state to prepare a plan to qualify for participation in some desirable state-funded program, or to receive certain state or federal grants. Smaller towns that want to have a general plan can get the job done with volunteers, some of their own paid staff, a temporary employee who can also work on other projects while working on the plan, a consultant, or any combination of these.

> *In addition to General Plans, some jurisdictions prepare what they call "Strategic Plans". There are few, if any, state statutes regarding strategic plans so these plans can contain anything. They vary from jurisdiction to jurisdiction, and are intended to focus on what the jurisdiction would like to have happen in the more immediate future to promote the jurisdiction's prosperity. Some people see the general plan framework as too constricting because it is often circumscribed by state law, so they take up strategic planning in addition to, or instead of, general planning. Often what is presented as a strategic plan might more simply be included as a part of a general plan. Examples of municipal strategic plans abound on the internet.*

Unless the state statutes require otherwise, city plans can be very general and just include a map with some brief associated text that indicates how the city council would like to have the city organized at some time in the future, usually 20 years hence. Some city plans are very extensive and contain a multitude of specific policies as well as descriptions of existing conditions, past trends, and forecasts.

City plans vary in legal status widely across the states. They can be strictly regulatory such that the city's zoning must be totally consistent with them; or, they can be conceptual such that they are virtually irrelevant to the zoning. How consistent they must be with zoning is something that is determined by state statute and case law. Before undertaking the preparation of any municipal general plan, you should have a clear understanding of how legally binding the statutes and case law have made your city plans.

> *In 1997 I served as the Planning Director for the Town of Paradise Valley, Arizona, one of the wealthiest towns in that state. On May 22, 1997, the Town adopted a new 15-page general plan that replaced its earlier general plan which contained more than ten times the pages. The 1997 Plan was written by the Town's planning staff with the help of a small citizens advisory committee, the town's planning commission, and the town council. The reason the town had a 15 page general plan was not because it couldn't afford more. It had a 15-page plan because the Town's leadership understood, the difference between prescription and description, and the value of common sense. They understood that if common sense told them that a certain issue was a problem (e.g. speeding on residential streets), and if another issue was not a problem (e.g. residential landscaping), then they didn't need to conduct a survey, or do a study to tell them about it. Similarly, the General Plan for the Town of Cave Creek, Arizona, was written a couple of years earlier in the same style. The value of a Plan is not related to its size; it is related to the impact the policy language it contains has on the improvement of the quality of life of the residents whose properties fall under its purview: "Policy language" refers to the plan's goals, objectives, policies, programs, activities, and actions. Verbosity in city plans can be a liability because it offers those who attack a plan's legality more openings into the plan upon which an attack can be focused.*

In some states, for example Oregon, plans have been given extremely binding legal status; e.g., an individual building permit can be invalidated solely on the basis of language in a plan. As a case in point, when I served as the county planning director for Benton County, Oregon, in the early 1980s, I authorized issuance of a farm-related building permit in an area designated on the county's general plan for agriculture. I thought the proposed dwelling met all the plan requirements, and it certainly met the zoning. Neighbors appealed my decision to the courts where the issuance of that building permit was invalidated on the basis of language contained in the Benton County, Oregon, General Plan at the time. On the other hand, as a planner working in the State of Connecticut, I not infrequently reviewed proposals for changes in zoning that blatantly ignored what the general plan called for in a particular area. In Connecticut, state general plans have had virtually no legal effectiveness other than to qualify public projects of a certain minimum cost for state funding support. In Oregon, city plans are adopted as law.

Whenever I read a city plan which has been written in the style of prescriptions jumbled up with descriptions, I use a bright colored highlighter to identify the prescriptions. This makes it much easier to understand what those who adopted the plan are urging others to do to help make the city a better place. Highlight any sentence anyplace in the document which includes phrases indicating that the city "should," or "must," or "encourages," or "discourages," or "supports," or "opposes," or intends to *do anything*. When you have completed that exercise the material you have highlighted is the actual plan. The remainder is simply information.

Plans can have some amount of information in them, but if more than ten percent of a plan document is descriptive information, your city would do its citizens a favor by removing most of the informational language. Just as a little spice in a scrambled egg, can actually help the digestion of the egg; a little descriptive material mixed in with the policy language of a city plan can help the policy language be understood. However, if the volume of spices on a scrambled egg exceeds the volume of the egg itself, the spices will make the entire mess indigestible. Similarly with the descriptive material in a city plan. This is not to say that the tests and analyses are not to be done; only that they should be assembled in a document separate from the plan itself.

It is common that, after a new plan is completed for a city, the zoning needs to be re-evaluated so that the zoning will properly implement the policy language contained in the new plan. A common relatively recent example of this relates to the treatment of residences in commercial zoning districts. Over the years, many cities have adopted zoning ordinances that have excluded residences from commercial zones to eliminate potential conflicts between those uses (e.g. heavy traffic, noises, night lights in commercial zones, etc.). However, by excluding residential uses from commercial zones cities have forced their residents into the suburbs and a drive to work, and have created downtowns that are dead at night and on weekends.

When considered from a planning perspective, a city council might determine that it would be better to allow residences in certain types of commercial areas, with certain limitations to reduce conflicts between the commercial and residential uses, such as limitations upon when commercial deliveries can be made. If, during the planning process, they reached that conclusion, and they included in their plan a policy statement that would encourage allowing residences in commercial zones, they would need to change their zoning to implement that policy.

General plans can be changed, amended. Usually state statutes regulate how often they can change and dictate the process that needs to be followed to adopt changes, but city plans are allowed to change. If the state statutes regulate such changes, the process that needs to be followed is generally more difficult than the process for amending a zoning ordinance because a general plan, in concept, is supposed to deal with a longer term view of the community than the zoning which should be more resistant to change.

Virtually every general plan contains a "land use" element that identifies the types of development the municipality intends to promote in what locations over the next ten or twenty years. This could simply be a replica of the map for the current zoning, or it could be something more creative that indicates the changes that the municipality would like to see take place in land use. If your state statutes require strict consistency between the zoning map and the general plan land use map, the safest way to handle the land use map is to have it replicate the zoning map.

WHY DO IT?

There are many reasons why the leadership of a city might want to agree to initiate the preparation of a city plan. It is very important to determine why you would want to have a city plan because that reason should play a strong role in determining the level of resources that you will want to dedicate to completing the plan.

IDEALISM/UTOPIANISM

There are idealistic reasons for preparing a city plan. In his 1974 book The Limits of the City, Murray Bookchin expresses one of those reasons as follows: "City planning finds its validation in the intuitive recognition that a burgeoning market society can not be trusted to produce spontaneously a habitable, sanitary, or even efficient city, much less a beautiful one."

Plans prepared for idealistic reasons have their own justification where cost can be a minor consideration in determining their scope. Such plans are prepared for people who sincerely believe that by explicitly describing and publicly agreeing upon the desired end state that they want their cities to reach, the residents of those cities will have more habitable, sanitary, efficient, and beautiful places to live. This is one of the higher ideal reasons for planning a city, and a reason that especially drives those who feel they know how to define such terms as "habitable, sanitary, efficient, and beautiful."

ISSUE PROMOTION

There are other interests that urge community leaders to prepare and adopt plans, such as those who believe that through such plans the government can have a stronger position in taking action to preserve the environment, provide better access to housing, promote racial integration, or accomplish whatever particular social, economic, or other objective the interest group desires to support. For a medical analogy, if the city planner prepares a prescription for a community like a doctor prepares a prescription for a patient, this group of advocates for planning could be compared to the drug and medical device manufacturers who would like to have prescriptions written that would promote the use of their products.

NEIGHBORHOOD ENHANCEMENT

Another group that can be found interested in planning is the group of those who feel that there is something about their neighborhood - in terms of urban design, or some other aspect - that they believe could be improved, and they become convinced that by looking at their neighborhood from a planning perspective they might get others to agree to do what it would take to have such improvements made.

POPULARITY
In addition to (1) those who honestly believe in the effectiveness of planning *a priori* ,(2) those who have an issue they want to promote, and (3) those who want changes to be made to their neighborhoods, there are (4) those who become supporters for the planning of their communities because people they admire seem to think it's a good idea and they want to associate with that group.

STATE OR FEDERAL MANDATES
Finally, there are those less idealistic supporters of planning who simply want the city to prepare a general plan so that it could qualify for special state and federal funding, activities, and programs. In a number of states - and the number of such states is growing - the state offers incentives to municipalities to encourage municipal planning. These incentives can be in the form of special grant programs for which municipalities with plans can qualify, or other such benefits that municipalities without plans will miss out on. In some states, the choice as whether to plan, or not to plan, has been completely taken out of the hands of the municipalities - those are the states that simply direct that its municipalities *will* prepare and adopt general plans.

INITIATING THE PLAN PREPARATION PROCESS

MOTIVATION

Many municipal comprehensive planning projects are initiated, not because of a groundswell of local interest, nor because of a need felt by community leadership, but because *the laws of the state in which the municipality exists encourage, or require such projects.*

Planning projects encouraged, or required by the state, are the easiest planning projects to complete, and they are also the ones that can result in the largest waste of municipal resources. To complete one of these projects, the very first thing that a municipality needs to do is to determine who will oversee the project: Will it be an experienced volunteer; a current staff person who could make time for the project by putting off some other responsibilities; a temporary employee hired to help complete the project, either full- or part-time; a consultant; or a local non-profit, educational institution, or regional planning, or other regional government agency (soil conservation district, economic development district, regional education district, etcetera)?

STAFFING

Often the easiest answer to the staffing question seems to be the hiring of a consultant, and that can be a very good way to get the job done. Consultants often have the experience necessary to expedite the process and to be able to assure you that all potential solutions to your planning issues have been brought up for consideration. On the other hand, sometimes consultants can go beyond what is needed for a minimalist plan so that the plan they prepare reflects as many of the consultant's skills as possible. That approach can run up the cost of a plan. On the good side, consultants generally can be relied upon to produce plans based on in-depth comprehensive analyses of all the issues related to the requirements for a general plan which are stated in the state statutes. On the downside, however, sometimes these analyses go beyond what the minimum requirements would dictate.

If your jurisdiction is primarily interested in preparing a plan that will qualify it to receive certain state funding, or to participate in certain state, or federally-funded programs, then all you need to do is to meet the minimum requirements, and generally these requirements are quite broadly stated in state statutes which leave much room for interpretation.

If a consultant is not the best choice for you, then you are generally left with finding an enthusiastic volunteer, using existing staff, or hiring a temporary employee, or finding an interested non-profit or regional special district government agency to do the work.

Finding an enthusiastic and able volunteer to do the "legwork" required to complete your planning project competently is not easy. If you happen to have a retiree with experience in public administration, you may be on to something. To find such an individual, you could ask your local newspaper to write a story about the project and have them include in the article an invitation for volunteers to contact you. You might also offer some type of remuneration to such an individual. You have to be willing and able to be creative if you want to take advantage of such an approach.

When I served as the Town Manager and Planning Director of the Town of Cave Creek, Arizona, through such a newspaper article I reached a retired school superintendent to whom I offered the minimum legal wage to write grant applications for the town. This arrangement worked wonderfully for several years and brought many, many times the cost of his minimum-wage hourly pay to the town in the form of grants he won for the town. This individual would have been totally competent to staff a general plan project for the town, if I had needed him to do that. This approach, however, will not be feasible for many towns because of the lack of willing, capable volunteers.

On the other hand, if the individual(s) your town currently has assigned to do planning, zoning, and/or building permit processing is enterprising and enthusiastic, then they may be excited about taking on the opportunity to staff your planning project as an additional workload assignment. This could be a learning opportunity, or a resume builder, if they are upwardly mobile professionally.

If, however, the individuals you have assigned to do planning, zoning, and/or building permit processing are more set in their interests, and are handling their current workload well for you, and they are not so interested in their professional upward mobility, then you may want to look for a temporary employee to do the staff work for the preparation of a new general plan for your municipality.

If your best option is to hire an intern, or a part-time, temporary employee, a good way to find an appropriate candidate would be to contact the state chapter of the American Planning Association (APA) for your state. These organizations often produce monthly, or quarterly newsletters in which you could put an advertisement, or a news story about your project with information about how interested persons could contact you. You could also contact the state chapter of the International City/County Management Association (ICMA) which could provide you with similar assistance.

In seeking a part-time, temporary employee you would either be seeking the type of individual I described earlier regarding volunteers, or a recent college graduate with an interest in government affairs, or maybe even directly in city planning. If you have a college in, or near your town, you might even be able to hire a student who would be able to take on a part-time job during the school year to serve as your planning project staff person.

If you follow this approach and hire a temporary planner recently out of college to provide staff support to the citizens' group responsible for preparing the plan, you would do well to encourage this staffer to attend as many conferences as possible that would relate to the needs of the town, and to focus on participating in as many conference workshops as possible that have some promise of funds that could be used to further town goals. New planners in such positions should also be encouraged to make an effort to meet the people giving presentations at the workshops so that they can remind them, if they communicate with them about a grant in the future, that they met at a certain conference.

> *If you are a bureaucrat in charge of giving out grants, you never want to be rightly accused by your boss of having given money to "some kook out there." By personally meeting the bureaucrats who give out grants, you can dispel some of that fear when they have to review a grant application that you submit. Being a successful grant jockey is a lot like being a salesman, you are more successful if you have the ability to glad-hand a lot of people to lubricate the grant processes you have to go through.*
>
> *Grantors themselves are people who work for someone who wants the grant program for which they are responsible to be successful. What if the legislative branch created and funded a grant program and no one applied for any of its grants? In the long run, the people who were hired to administer the program would no longer have a job. This is not all that far-fetched a situation.*
>
> *There are federal grant funds every year that go begging, not for any fault of the bureaucrats who are administering them. Grantors are always looking for "good" jurisdictions to which they can award their grant funds so that their jobs will be assured. If they can't get rid of their money, they can be replaced by someone who can; or, the program itself can be scrapped - especially if the legislators who originally concocted the program have lost their elections and are no longer in office. If your employee can get a reputation for administering grant programs without scandal, confusion, or delay, the employee can become a grantsman and can get on a band wagon that will result in calls from grantors telling the employee to apply for grants which have*

more money available than there are applicants. Once your grantsman has that happen, he can bring money to your jurisdiction with greatly diminished effort and increased success.

Writing a general plan for a smaller town is not rocket science - it is more like backyard gardening and most people, given a little time, can do it. A recent college graduate with good writing skills and a desire to make a mark in the planning field can do an excellent job helping a committee of citizens prepare a very good plan for a smaller town. Then, if the person has been given the resources to find grant funding for town projects, the person could be kept on the payroll for the purpose of continuing to find grants. It is a sad truth that there is an extraordinary flow of grants from the federal, and most state governments as politicians exhaust themselves trying to show how much they care for their constituents and for the causes they feel are popular. While grants come with particular requirements for achieving certain goals, they can often be focused so that, even if their primary stated goal is not one your town would be interested in achieving, they can be used in part, at least, to achieve a goal your town is interested in - if nothing more than qualifying to receive a follow-up grant with more flexibility in its application.

You might be concerned that a student studying public administration, or planning, or political science at a local college might not be qualified to provide you with the planning services you need to produce an acceptable general plan for your town. You might feel you need to hire a "professional Planner" to do the job.

Many people would consider me a "Professional Planner". I have a master's degree in planning from a reputable school - the Maxwell School of Citizenship and Public Affairs of Syracuse University - and more than 45 years of experience in local government, including more than two decades as a Planning Director, or staff planner for half a dozen municipalities, and another couple of years as a planning consultant for a sole proprietary firm I created called Practical Planning Services. I could certainly serve a small town, or a large town for that matter, as its planning staff person, but for the great majority of smaller towns, although it might be helpful in expediting their planning process, my skills and experience would be much more than what would be needed.

The special contribution that I - or a person with a similar background - would bring to your planning project would be experience and training that would enable me to present you with ideas, alternatives, and concepts, which might interest you, but which a less experienced, less well trained person might not be able to bring to such a project. However, if you are simply interested in meeting the minimum requirements to qualify your town to receive state, federal, or foundation grants - which is a perfectly worthy goal at the outset - then you don't need an individual of my caliber to do the job. Maybe after you have completed the project, if you had the extra time and funding, you could hire a professional consultant to review your work and provide you with suggestions for additional goals, objectives, policies, and/or programs to refine your work, but that would be a completely optional decision.

To wrap this discussion up, I want to give you one relatively simple example of the kind of thing a professional planner could do for you. In the late 1970s I worked as the senior planner for the City of Albany, Oregon. In that capacity I was able to help the City write it's general plan, re-write its zoning laws, and review development proposals submitted by property owners. The owner of a property, part of which is now identified as 3263 Southwest Lyon Street, wanted to build 6 homes on his vacant property.

The property is located on a curve such that his surveyor brought in a design for the subdivision of the property into six pie-shaped lots with very, very long skinny driveways, one right next to another. With the little bit of professional experience I had at that time, I suggested that, instead of six long skinny driveways all next to each other, he should divide the property leaving a circular landscaped island in front of the lots, with six shorter driveways coming off the circle (sometimes referred to as an "eyebrow").

The owner took the suggestion, and, if you google that location today, you can see how the design worked out - to me it looks pretty good. I give this small example because it is easy to comprehend, not because that is the only type of contribution professional planning experience can bring to a planning project. Professional planning assistance can be helpful to any jurisdiction, but may not be what is required for the product your town may be seeking.

For an analogy, a professional manicurist can doubtless do a better job clipping my toenails than I can, but ordinarily I don't really need a better job than what I can do.

Thus, the first action you need to take to start your general plan preparation project is to determine who you are going to have serve as the staff person to do the "leg work" to keep the project moving: Find a good volunteer or intern, invite an interested member of your current staff to take on this new assignment, or hire a part-time temporary student, or recent graduate student in planning or a related field. As a last-ditch choice you could also consider a part-time temporary un-, or under-employed, individual with a degree in planning or a related field; or, finally, you may wish to simply turn the project over to a planning consultant.

There are two other options that may also work for your town, but these are only available if your are located in an area that is served by a regional non-profit or regional special district organization.

Councils of Government & Regional Planning Organizations
In addition to an office that prepares a general plan for the state in which you are located - a state planning office, which many states have - some states also have regional planning organizations (often identified as "councils of government") that cover most, if not all, of the state. Some of these will provide planning consulting services, and some of these services can be offered at a cost much lower than private consulting services (although some provide such services at the equivalent of private consulting company rates). If your jurisdiction is covered by a regional planning organization which is capable of providing planning services to local jurisdictions, contracting with that organization for staffing help may be a very good option for you.

Educational Institution and Others
If your town is located within commuting distance of a college or university that offers a planning, or related degree program, you may be

ideally situated to take advantage of an opportunity that might only cost you for materials, and some reimbursements for mileage. As a graduate assistant in the master's degree program in which I was enrolled in the 1960s, I was responsible for finding suitable annual projects for the graduate students in planning to complete as a team. One such project was a plan for the redevelopment of the core area of the City of Utica, New York. That plan was very well received by the City Council and served for years as a foil to help the Council review subsequent specific redevelopment proposals submitted by private developers. A nearby college or university could provide you with at least the skeleton of a plan that could be used to create a complete general plan for your municipality, often at a small portion of the cost that a private consultant would charge.

Finally, there are soil and water conservation districts, and other special district governments in different places across the country. Sometimes their staffs are available to help smaller jurisdictions prepare their general plans for a modest amount. If you are unfamiliar with the special districts in your area you can check your tax bill to see which ones you are paying taxes to. In some areas a regional chamber of commerce might be interested in working with a town to prepare a city plan for a fee.

Finally, a general comment regarding the employment of professional planners whether as consultants or employees. Just as many health professionals did not accept acupuncture as a legitimate medical practice for a long time, planning professionals have their own biases. For example, the national professional organization for planners (the American Planning Association, APA) opposes the use of cul-de-sac subdivision design, and the majority of professional planners bring that bias to their work. Some planners, myself included, support the use of the cul-de-sac, and we even live, or have lived on cul-de-sac roads. If you do hire a professional planner to staff your project, or even to review the work you have done without a professional planner, you need to continue to use your common sense and not allow the attitudes of the professional to turn your plan into a document that reflects their biases more than you actually want. Professionals will be helpful, but they also have their biases.

> *For those who object to the cul-de-sac because of the interruption it gives to thru traffic circulation, there is a much*

> better solution than the standard grid street system: It is called The Fused Grid Street System. For information about that alternative, see <u>REMAKING THE CITY STREET GRID - A Model for Urban and Suburban Development</u> by Fanis Grammenos and G.R. Lovegrove published by McFarland Press in 2015. http://www.mcfarlandbooks.com/book-2.php?id=978-0-7864-9604-4

Professional planners do have unique training and skills to contribute to plan preparation projects. Planners generally, myself included, advocate allowing residential uses in the commercial zones so that commercial areas can have more round-the-clock activity patterns, and for other community style of life benefits. That is a real asset that many towns have precluded for themselves through their zoning, and which virtually all professional planners would recommend. That is only one example of a valuable idea a professional planner would likely bring to your project.

> As the Town Manager/Planning Director of Gila Bend, Arizona, in the late 1990s, I received an application from the owner of the town's only grocery store (50 miles to the nearest full-service grocery store) to rebuild the store and greatly expand it, which would have been a tremendous asset to the town. The store had originally been built before the town had zoning, and the owner's residence was above the store. He wanted to rebuild a greatly enlarged grocery store and continue to have his residence above the store. I was thrilled with this prospect, although the town's zoning ordinance prohibited such a mix of uses. I recommended that the Planning Commission amend the zoning ordinance to allow some mixed uses, such as the one this owner had proposed, but I was roundly chastised by the chair of the commission on the grounds that she had found that most small towns in Arizona did not permit such mixed uses. The proposal failed and for years thereafter the town's residents had to continue to either drive into the Phoenix Metro Area for a full-service grocery, or to reduce their expectations and enjoy the meager offerings of their little old grocery store. Sometimes the advice of a professional planner can be very constructive.

PART III - THE CITIZENS' ADVISORY COMMITTEE

COMMITTEE PROTOCOL

Now that you have determined how you are going to staff your general plan project, you need to set up a structure that will help you ensure that the product you and your staff will produce will be broadly acceptable to the public. The traditional and most effective way to do that is to have the project overseen by a citizens' advisory committee.

Citizens advisory committees can be a great blessing or a dread curse to any project. In the best case, they can support and encourage community-wide acceptance of a project. However, I have also seen them in their worst case in which their members became active opponents of the governing body that appointed them, even as far as running for office to depose them! This is not what you want from your citizens committees, and, especially not from a citizens committee working on a general plan preparation project.

COMMITTEE STRUCTURE

There is never a guarantee that the citizens committee you establish will not turn against you, but by structuring the committee so that it's role in the planning process is clearly understood by everyone from the beginning, you can greatly increase the chances that your committee will be a positive, contributing member of the general plan preparation team.

Following is a template with commentary (followed by a clean version of the same template) for a draft set of simple but effective bylaws for your citizens' committee which I wrote for the ICMA in 1996 and which still provides an excellent structure for such committees (reprinted by permission, from "Establishing Effective Citizens' Advisory Committees," MIS Report, Vol. 28, No. 2, February 1996, copyright © ICMA). Using these bylaws will help you avoid many hazards inherent in establishing a new committee, and will give the new committee a great advantage over committees established without bylaws.

BYLAWS TEMPLATE WITH COMMENTARY

Article I. Name

The name of this committee is the ___(name) and it shall also be known as the (acronym)_ .

> *Every citizens' committee should have an official name and acronym to be used by the governing body, the committee members, the staff, the press and the public. Without a name people will invent different names and acronyms for the committee which will create confusion.*

Article II. Purpose, Authority, Duties, and Termination

A. The purpose of this committee is to advise the ___(governing body of the city, town, or coullty) __ about matters relating to _____ and specifically whether the ___(city, town, county) __ _ should or not _____.

> *The most important section of the bylaws for any citizens' committee is the statement of purpose. The purpose of any committee is to take the time to analyze in detail a particular subject and to provide considered recommendations to the governing body for action. Without a clear statement of purpose, the committee may begin to imagine itself to be the decision-making authority; it may consider part of its purpose to be confrontation with the governing body; or, it may think it was appointed to direct the governing body. The statement of purpose helps the staff and governing body think about the purpose of the committee. It isolates and identifies the problem. Governing bodies will sometimes think they need a committee to address a problem when different members of the governing body have very different ideas about what the problem is and why and how long it should be studied. The statement of purpose also requires agreement among a majority of the members of the governing body about the purpose of the committee. If the governing body cannot reach agreement about the purpose of a citizens' committee, then it is good to stop the process at that time to avoid getting a committee started at all. A potentially truly disastrous citizens' committee is one that doesn't even have the governing body agreeing about its purpose.*

B. The committee's authority and existence will terminate when its recommendations have been presented to the council, or on _(date)_, whichever occurs first. The ___(governing body) __ may determine to continue the existence of this committee by amending these bylaws.

> *In addition to an overall program development or project development objective, some committees also have specific ongoing duties assigned to them, such as the duty to review the environmental impact statements of all proposed road construction projects. If this were their only function, the committee would better be called a "commission" and would not need to have a termination date. A termination date in the bylaws is a convenient way to give everyone a general idea of just how in-depth the background and analysis work of the committee is intended to be. A termination date also reminds committee members that they are not the governing body.*

Article III. Membership
A. There will be _____ members on the committee. Each member of the governing body shall appoint one member to the committee and that committee member shall serve at the pleasure of the governing body member by whom they were appointed and shall serve no longer than that governing body member serves on the governing body.

> Second only in importance to the statement of purpose is the statement regarding the composition of a committee's membership. There is much confusion about committee membership and how it should be determined. Local government committees are formed to advise the governing body that appoints them. These committees should not be confused with interest groups that lobby local governments. Lobbying groups have their purpose and they will work to achieve them. Citizens' advisory committees to the governing body of a local government have one purpose - to increase the governing body's ability to deal with complex issues. When the governing body does not have enough time to deal with an issue directly itself, it is appropriate to secure volunteer assistance in the form of a citizens' committee.
>
> Because such committee's advise the governing body, often the best way to determine who should be on the committee is for every member of the governing body to pick one member. In that way, the political spectrum of the elected governing body is maintained by the citizens' committee, and the recommendations of the committee will have a better chance of being accepted by the governing body. By composing the committee in this way, every member of the governing body has a direct connection to the work of the committee. This arrangement assures that such committees always reflect the composition of the governing body.
>
> An alternative selection method is for the entire governing body to select each member of the committee by majority vote. Such a selection process tends to form a committee in the image of the majority of the council, which in some cases is politically desired, but which may create problems if minority views from the governing body are not reflected at all on the advisory committee.
>
> Efforts to select committee members on the basis of some abstract concept of "balance" on the various sides of an issue are difficult because the majority of the governing body is often perceived as "loading" such committees and therefore the recommendations of such committees are less likely to be well

> received. Such efforts can be very time consuming and controversial.
>
> Some citizens' committees are established to address a specific question over which several organized groups may be in dispute. In such situations it may be useful to establish an ad hoc committee of representatives of the groups involved to try to mediate an acceptable solution. Such a committee could benefit from a written set of bylaws but would not have the kind of membership recommended for a citizens' committee dealing with a more general community issue.
>
> Also included in this section of the bylaws is the stipulation that the members of the committee serve "at the pleasure" of the member of the governing body who appointed them. This gives the members of the governing body the right to remove their appointees for any reason at any time and assures that the committee will be sensitive to the concerns of the members of the governing body who appointed them. Without that phrase in the membership section of the bylaws, governing bodies expose themselves to the possibility of having a lawsuit filed against them if they try to remove a committee member, and of having to prove in court that there was some "just cause" for which the member should be removed (in some cases the courts have found that membership on a citizenship committee can constitute a "property right").
>
> Often governing bodies limit membership on their advisory committees to residents, or registered voters, or business or property owners in the jurisdiction. That is a matter of individual preference.

B. Vacancies are filled in the same manner as the original appointments.
C. Upon failure of any member to attend three consecutive meetings, the committee may recommend that the governing body terminate that appointment and declare the position vacant, to be filled in the manner of a regular appointment.

> In addition to having the clause that allows the appointing authority to remove a member from an advisory committee, it is also useful to have a section in the committee bylaws that allows the committee itself to recommend removal of one of its members for failure to attend committee meetings.

Article IV. Officers and Staffing
A. Officers. The officers consist of a chair and vice chair who shall be selected by the membership and who shall serve at the pleasure of the

membership for one-year terms. Officers may be re-elected.

B. Chair. The chair shall have general supervisory and directional powers over the committee. The chair shall preside at all committee meetings and set committee agendas. The chair shall also be an ex-officio member of all subcommittees and shall be the sole spokesperson for the committee unless this responsibility is delegated in writing.

Handling committee member and public comments is the responsibility of the chair, unless the chair chooses an approach that a majority of the committee disagrees with. If that occurs, a member of the committee may either suggest a different approach to the chair, or make a motion that would be binding, if passed, on the chair to require that a different approach be taken. Regarding public comments it should be remembered that the meetings of the committee are just that, meetings of the committee. The fact that state law will require them to be open to the public does not mean that the public has the same right to speak at the meetings as the members of the committee do. The public must be able to observe the meeting, but not necessarily to participate in the business of the meeting. Unless it would be helpful to do otherwise, the best way to handle public comments is to follow one of two procedures:

Accept public comments only when the committee reaches an item listed on the agenda.

Accept public comment only after committee members have completed their discussion of an agenda item, but before a vote is taken on it.

In either case, the public should be advised of the procedure to be followed.

C. Vice Chair. The vice chair shall execute all powers of the chair in the absence of the chair.

D. Staff. The jurisdiction will provide staff support to the committee for meeting notification, typing, copying, and information gathering to the extent that the budget permits.

To operate effectively, every committee needs a chair and a vice chair. Occasionally, the governing body may wish to choose the chair, but it is usually more effective to permit the members of the committee to select its own officers. The officers' principal responsibility is to facilitate the operation of the committee, and usually the members themselves are the best judges of who would be the best person to perform that function. The members of the committee need to have the authority to replace their leadership if they are not satisfied with their performance; the phrase "at the pleasure of the membership" provides for that authority and keeps the chair in a position of service to, rather than dominance over, the committee.

The officers need to know how long they will hold office and whether they can hold the same office repeatedly. Committees that work on major construction-related projects may require more than a year to see their projects completed, so it is not unusual for officers on such committees to be re-elected.

The officers of any committee also need to know what authority they have to speak on behalf of the committee. A committee will have trouble if multiple voices claim to speak on its behalf. By specifically designating the chairman to perform this function, the bylaws can minimize this problem.

Of all the responsibilities described for the various officers, the most important one for the committee is the chair's responsibility to set the agenda. When the bylaws do not specify who has this authority, lengthy debates can ensue over that question.

The chair needs to know what agencies will provide staff support. These proposed bylaws call for the staff to perform a number of secretarial functions for the committee. If the jurisdiction is not able to provide that type of support, it may be wise to forego the formation of a committee until adequate staff support is available.

Article V. Organizational Procedures

A. The committee shall hold meetings as necessary at a time and place designated by the chair, or in cases of disagreement, by majority vote of the membership.

B. Fifty-one percent of the voting membership of the committee shall constitute a quorum.

C. These bylaws may be repealed or amended, or new bylaws may be adopted by a majority vote of the governing body on its own initiative, or upon a recommendation from the committee.

D. The parliamentary authority for this committee is <u>Robert's Rules of Order Revised</u>, except where superseded by these bylaws or local, state, or federal law.

In addition to members and officers, every committee needs some organizational procedures to minimize confusion about when and where they are going to meet, and about who is responsible to decide such things.

A quorum is the minimum number of members necessary to conduct committee business. A quorum of less than 50 percent of the membership is not good because -depending upon the size of the committee - it may allow as small as a 25 percent portion of the members to take action on behalf of the committee. A quorum of more than 50 percent assures that at least 43 percent (three people on a committee of seven members) must approve of a decision, which helps ensure that no extraordinarily inconsistent action is taken at a poorly attended meeting.

Another procedure that needs to be specified is the amendment of the committee's bylaws. Amendments should always require the concurrence of the governing body that appointed the committee. Bylaws that are changed frequently can destabilize the work of a committee, especially if they are not approved by the governing body. A final rule that should be set for any committee regards the determination of the committee's parliamentary authority. Parliamentary procedures are to public meetings what manners are to mealtimes; they are designed to assure courtesy and respect among the participants. The most commonly used parliamentary authority is <u>Robert's Rules of Order Revised.</u> There are other simpler authorities that are especially useful for small committees, but so few people are familiar with them that it is usually more trouble than it is worth to designate something other than Robert's Rules. Many people are unfamiliar with parliamentary procedure and therefore feel uncomfortable serving on committees, but lack of knowledge about parliamentary procedure need not be a problem. The League of Women Voters and many other public agencies and nonprofit *organizations provide good introductions to parliamentary procedure, in the form of books and pamphlets, as well as audio and video tapes. Simple introductory materials should be provided to all committee members as needed.*

BYLAWS TEMPLATE MODEL

Article I. Name The name of this committee is the __(name) and it shall also be known as the (acronym)_ .

Article II. Purpose, Authority, Duties, and Termination
    A. The purpose of this committee is to advise the ___(governing body of the city, town, or coul1ty) __ about matters relating to _____ and specifically whether the ___(city, town, county) __ _ should or not _____.
    B. The committee's authority and existence will terminate when its recommendations have been presented to the council, or on _ (date) __ , whichever occurs first. The __(governing body) __ may determine to continue the existence of this committee by amending these bylaws.

Article III. Membership
    A. Each member of the governing body shall appoint one member to the committee and that committee member shall serve at the pleasure of the governing body member by whom he or she was appointed and shall serve no longer than that governing body member serves on the governing body.
    B. Vacancies are filled in the same manner as the original appointments.
    C. Upon failure of any member to attend three consecutive meetings, the committee may recommend termination of that appointment to the governing body and the governing body may remove the incumbent from the committee, and declare the position vacant to be filled in the manner of a regular appointment.

Article IV. Officers and Staffing
    A. Officers. The officers consist of a chair and a vice chair who shall be selected by the membership and who shall serve at the pleasure of the membership for ___(number)_ year terms. Officers may be re-elected.
    B. Chair. The chair shall have general supervisory and directional powers over the committee. The chair shall preside at all committee meetings and set committee agendas. The chair shall also be an ex-officio member of all subcommittees and shall be the sole spokesperson for the committee unless this responsibility is delegated in writing.
    C. Vice Chair. The vice chair shall execute all powers of the chair in the absence of the chair.

D. Staff. The _(jurisdiction)_ will provide staff support to the committee for meeting notification, typing, copying, and information gathering to the extent that the budget permits.

Article V. Organizational Procedures

A. The committee shall hold meetings as necessary at a time and place designated by the chair, or in cases of disagreement, by majority vote of the membership.

B. Fifty-one percent of the voting membership of the committee shall constitute a quorum.

C. These bylaws may be repealed or amended, or new bylaws may be adopted at any time by a majority vote of the _ (governing body)_ on its own initiative, or upon a recommendation from the committee.

D. The parliamentary authority for this committee is <u>Robert's Rules of Order Revised</u>, except where superseded by these bylaws or local, state, or federal law.

COMMITTEE STARTUP

You will need the following materials to get your committee started:

LETTER OF INVITATION TO THE MEMBERS:
>Dear
>On behalf of all citizens of ___ (name of jurisdiction)_ , I would like to
>congratulate you on your appointment to the
>_____ Committee.
>
>___ (Name of staff member) _ , of the _____
>Department, who is your staff liaison, will serve as your primary contact with City Hall and should be able to answer most questions or address any concerns you may have. As a committee member, you are also encouraged to contact the Mayor and Council at any time with specific concerns, issues, or questions.
>
>Enclosed is a copy of your committee's bylaws, a membership roster, some information about the state's laws regarding open meetings and conflict of interest, a summary of Roberts' Rules of Order, Revised, which is the committee's parliamentary authority, and an agenda for your committee's first meeting, which is scheduled for:
>>Date:
>>Time:
>>Location:
>
>Again, thank you for your willingness to serve. It is our hope that your experience on this committee will be both interesting and productive. We look forward to working with you.
>Yours very truly,
>Mayor _____ _

>>Attachments - Agenda for the first meeting
>>Information on your state's open meeting law
>>Information on your state's conflict of interest laws
>>Summary overview of Robert's Rules of Order, Revised
>>(or other parliamentary authority)

AGENDA TEMPLATE FOR THE FIRST MEETING

Agenda

Meeting of the ___ (name of jurisdiction) ___ Citizens' Advisory Committee on the __ (subject of the committee) __ _

Date: _____ Time: _____ Location: ____

1. Call to order, welcome and introductions - Member of the City Council

The first meeting of any new citizens' committee should be called to order by the mayor, or at least a member of the city council. Along with the call to order, should be a welcome and introduction of all the members and the staff that will be working with them. An overview of the jurisdiction's organization chart and a budget summary could also be helpful.

2. Approval of the minutes of the previous meeting (to be handled at the next meeting)
3. Review of correspondence
4. Consideration of Business
    a. Election of Officers (to be handled at the next meeting)

There are basically two ways to elect officers: A motion can be made to select a certain individual as the chair; the motion can be seconded, and voted on and, if it passes, the committee has a chair. If it does not pass, another motion can be made for a different individual, seconded, and so forth until a chair is elected. In the second method of electing officers, nominations are declared open by the individual conducting the meeting and names of nominees are written on a blackboard. Then the members are asked one-by-one to cast their vote. If one member receives a majority of the votes, he or she is elected chair. If not, the committee should take a brief recess and address the matter again after the recess. Because committee decisions are made by majority vote of the members, if no member receives votes from a majority of the committee members, no one has been elected. For instance, on a seven-member committee if three people run for chair and two people each receive two votes and one receives three votes, no one has yet been elected. After the chair has been elected, the gavel should be passed to the chair, who should then conduct the election of the vice chair and the remainder of the meeting.

5. Setting of regular meeting days and times
6. Briefings
    a. Bylaws
    b. Conflict of interest laws

State conflict of interest laws should be reviewed so that no committee member will accidentally participate in the discussion of a matter that would involve them in a conflict of interest. Such matters generally relate to contracts or projects that could benefit them, or their immediate family members, in a direct way. For instance, if a citizens' committee is preparing to recommend a company to maintain park landscaping in the town and a member of the committee owns a landscape company that has bid on the service, that member should declare a conflict of interest and abstain from any discussion of, or voting on that recommendation.

      c.   Open meeting law

State laws contain "open meeting" laws that that require that groups such as formally appointed citizens' committees hold their meetings in a location that is open to the public. These laws usually also require that notice of any meeting be posted in a public place at least 24 hours before the meeting of such a group.

      d.   parliamentary procedure guidelines
7.   Other business
8.   Comments from the public
9.   Comments from committee members
10.   Other
11.   Adjournment

PART IV - THE SUBSTANCE OF PLANNING

"A shoe is not only a design, but it's a part of your body language, the way you walk. The way you're going to move is quite dictated by your shoes."
>   Christian Louboutin, a French shoe designer

To paraphrase Louboutin:
>   A city is not only a design, but it's a part of that which creates your life, the way you live. The way you're going to move is quite dictated by your city.

With your staff and committee you are now ready to do the work of preparing the Plan. There are many ways to do this. A traditional way is to undertake a comprehensive research effort to attempt to describe the current situation of the city as completely as possible in terms of who lives in it, works in it, plays in it, etc., as well as the current condition of the roads, parks, rivers, forests, etc., etc., and past trends that have gotten the city to where it is today, and forecasts for the future. This information is frequently published as a "Background Information Report" so that it doesn't have to encumber the General Plan itself, which should be a pretty clean policy document.

There's nothing wrong with having a Background Information Report, but, depending upon what you want out of your plan, you may not need to do all that work. Common sense may tell you most of what you need to know in relation to writing your plan's goals, objectives, policies, programs, actions and activities (GOPPAAs). Furthermore, a plan can be amended such that if you did leave something critical out because of a lack of information, you can always amend the plan to bring in additional language later.

Thus, an alternative way to initiate the development of your general plan is to have your staff prepare a draft template for the plan which would outline the plan elements to be included, and maybe even give a goal or two, and maybe even some objectives for each element. With that template presented to the General Plan Advisory Committee (GPAC) the GPAC could divide itself into sub-committees to further "flesh out" the plan by giving it additional goals, objectives, etcetera.

If you are doing a plan to meet minimum requirements, you may not need to spend a lot of time doing this work. You may also encounter an issue that does require some detailed information that either a member of the committee, or the staff, could research. The results of such research should be included in a document so that it can conveniently be made available to the public, and this could be your Background Information Report (BIR). Your BIR could be a very brief document, or something larger, if that were needed.

If you want your plan to contain graphics, such as a land use or transportation element map, you may wish to contract with a consultant to prepare those for you so that they will be clear and professional looking. The two plans included in the Appendices of this book were written before such mapping was commonly available and for that reason their mapping is not included in this book. If I were doing those plans today the mapping for them would have been contracted out.

Depending upon the size of your municipality, the work of drafting your GOPPAs should not extend over more than a period of a few months. Depending upon the type of community you live in, after that work has been done, you should have a document that can be given to the community at-large for comments, final changes made, and the end product presented to your Planning Commission and City Council (unless your state statutes require otherwise) for required public hearings and final adoption.

Some people like to have a "vision" statement as the opening narrative in their general plan. There is nothing wrong with having a vision statement, but neither is there to having no vision statement. If the exercise of preparing a vision statement - which is a statement about the characteristics of the type of community you collectively would like your community to be a couple of decades from now - then preparing a vision statement might be a good exercise for your city. If, on the other hand, you are interested in completing a plan that meets minimum requirements for the state or federal opportunity you want to be able to take advantage of, and if they don't require a vision statement, then you are fine to leave your plan without a vision statement.

For information, an Appendix to this book includes a copy of the 1993 General Plan of the Town of Cave Creek, Arizona, which was prepared using the processes described in this book. Although state laws and the physical, political, social and natural environments have changed since that plan was adopted, the model it gives is still illustrative of what can be done to meet state requirements to prepare a general plan for a municipality when resources are limited and other needs deserve priority.

If your city allows high density apartments and condominiums in commercial zones, you have the potential for a very different type of lifestyle than you do if you live in a city that does not permit those things.

The same can be said of allowing residences above businesses, street intersections as roundabouts, sidewalks set back from streets to leave landscape strips, duplex housing on street corners, cul-de-sac streets, and any other design alternative you can imagine. Regarding any imaginable option, there is no single prescribed approach. Virtually any approach can be chosen and be made to work, if that is the preference of the populace. There are very few absolutes in planning. Cul-de-sacs should be large enough to allow large sized emergency vehicles to turn around. Residential cul-de-sacs should not be so long as to cause unreasonable traffic entering and exiting during rush hours. Streets should be designed using standard measurements, although parking can be prohibited on streets to allow them to be significantly narrowed.

In planning your city you can choose to include policies regarding as many of the subjects noted above as you choose, or you can have a bare bones plan that ignores all those and other unusual policies in deference to past practice, if past practice has met your needs.

Depending upon how much you want to diverge from past practice, if you wish you may want to contract with a planning professional to help you envision different options for how your city might be guided to develop in the future. Otherwise, you should meet with your committee, your friends and associates and prepare the best plan you are able to and call your work done. The following section will give you some tips on that part of the process.

PART V - THE LAW

OVERVIEW

Now that you have a staff person, and a citizens' committee to provide direction to the project and to review the staff's work, the project is ready to begin.

The first thing that needs to be done: Staff needs to advise the state's office responsible for planning (if there is one) that the project is about to get underway and to ask the state if it has any resources (information, funding, staff assistance, etc.) that would be helpful. The same contact should be made with the regional planning organization that covers the area in which the municipality lies.

Staff also needs to join the state chapter of the American Planning Association (APA), and to plan to attend the next annual conference of the chapter. The annual conference will be a good source of information about what others in the state have done, and what changes in state laws, guidelines, and case law about planning have recently, or are potentially going to occur. It wouldn't hurt for the staff to also plan to attend the annual conference of the National APA, to meet others working on similar projects and exchange ideas with them.

INTERPRETATION OF STATE STATUTES

The staff should make a copy of the state's statutes regarding planning (to the extent that they exist) to determine what the state requires for it to accept a municipal plan. The state may only require procedural steps in terms of hearings that must be held, or it may require certain content in the plan. This is very important information, however, it should not be over-interpreted; no more should be read into the statutes than what they say. For example, a state statute may require that a plan "address the issue of homelessness." If that's all the statute says about it, and if there is no case law that gives any further refinement of that requirement, then that's the requirement. The response to the requirement could be as simple as a sentence in the plan stating that, for example, "the policies in this plan were written to address the issue of homelessness to the extent feasible." In many cases, unless you are told otherwise directly by someone in a state position of authority (and even such a person may not actually have the authority to be directive on such a matter), that may be all that is needed to satisfy the state requirement that your plan "address the issue of homelessness."

I repeat, you don't need to over-interpret what the state statutes say. You need to read the statutes literally until you are told literally, specifically, and directly, by someone who has authority - ultimately the Governor's Office - that there is a more refined interpretation of the statutes to which your plan must respond before the state will accept it, if you are preparing a plan that you wish to have the state accept. And, even if you get such a note and it comes under the authority of the Governor's Office, you don't have to accept it without a challenge.

At this point it is important to recognize what state statutes are.

Once the state statutes on any matter are adopted by the legislative branch, they begin to be interpreted by the executive and judicial branches. The executive branch interprets them in the form of Executive Orders, rules, regulations, and guidelines published by the various executive departments. These orders declare how the executive branch will treat ambiguities in the statutes.

State statutes are laws written by your state legislators. These legislators have a multitude of motives for voting for legislation, and they represent very broad constituencies. The process of writing legislation can be very convoluted and complex such that a state legislator who sponsors a bill may not even recognize the bill he sponsored when it comes out of the various committees and is eventually signed into law. Along the way other legislators hang their pet legislative changes on the bill like a Christmas tree, deals are made to modify language, parts of the bill are deleted, until a bill finally becomes law. As a result, language such as "municipal plans must address the issue of homelessness" gets introduced and adopted as state law. This language may have been inserted at the behest of some influential state legislator who has subsequently been defeated at the polls by another legislator who has no interest in the subject, and the Governor may have no interest in bringing up the subject either because he doesn't have a vote-winning solution to the problem. Therefore, even though the "state" may at one time have had an interest in having all municipal plans "address the issue of homelessness", there may be no one in a position of authority in the state who will do anything about your plan if you choose to address the issue of homelessness in the most superficial way. If that's the case, and it will not infrequently be the case because the attention spans, and political careers, of state legislators can be short, then all you need in your plan is the phrase "address the issue of homelessness" and you will probably have met the requirement.

Beyond that, if some Executive Branch official who isn't in close touch with the Governor's Office about the issue, attempts to require you to do more, you can always contact your state representative or state senator and tell them to speak with the bureaucrat about the matter, or to get the Governor's Office to help you in relation to the issue.

Here's an example. Several years ago in Connecticut, the Executive Branch issued a directive that the state would only support Federal recognition of Economic Development Districts (EDD) that covered at least 15 municipalities. The Federal EDD designation carries certain economic benefits with it and cannot be granted without the support of the Governor. The EDD I was working for only covered 7 municipalities. I was told repeatedly by a dedicated, well-meaning career bureaucrat that the Governor would not give his approval to our application for a Federal EDD until we added more municipalities to our EDD, which our governing board did not want to do. We applied for the EDD over the bureaucrat's objection with the support of one of our state legislators, and the Governor signed our application! And the "Feds" promptly approved it as well! The moral of the story is that it can be helpful to recognize that the Executive Branch of government is not necessarily a monolithic decision-making authority. More properly speaking it is an assortment of decision-making authorities subject to constant interpretation and deal-making. If your state legislator has something to offer the Governor, and you need some help on some state or federal grant or program, your state legislator can certainly give you a good shot at getting the relief you need, regardless of other Executive Branch ruminations about the subject.

For another example, I worked for more than a dozen years with councils of governments in Connecticut. During all that time the state statutes clearly stated that to be a voting member of a council of governments governing board, you had to be an *elected* official. Virtually all of the councils of governments in the state blatantly violated that statute for years by allowing *appointed* officials to vote on their governing boards, and nothing was ever done to correct it. Literally thousands of decisions made by those councils of governments were made illegally, but, because there was no constituency to challenge those decisions, nothing was ever done to correct the situation. This is just one example of the slippage that occurs between the adoption of legislation by the legislative branch and the administration of the legislation by the executive branch.

It's important to be aware of this "slippage" when you are a small town trying to prepare a plan to meet the requirements of a state statute so that you don't over-react to what the executive branch is actually enforcing from what the statutes require. The legislature adopts statutes through a complicated process of give-and-take. The final wording of state legislation reflects the myriad compromises required for it to garner the votes needed to get it passed. Then even when it is signed into law, the Executive Branch may simply choose not to enforce it.

The various constituencies that fought to get wording into the legislation change as members of the legislature lose elections and their replacements take office, so that wording that once seemed important to someone, now doesn't have anyone particularly interested in it any longer. That's what happened to the requirement that the voting members of the Connecticut councils of government had to be elected officials. After a while no legislator cared if they were, or were not, elected officials, and no one wanted to call attention to the problem by proposing to change the statutes; so that part of the statutes was simply ignored by everyone for decades.

In summary, one of the first things to do to start your project should be to collect copies of all executive branch interpretations of the state planning statutes, including opinions of the state attorney general. This collection shouldn't comprise more than a dozen or so pages of materials. For example, in relation to city plans, the state housing office may issue a guideline that states that for it to certify that the plan has addressed diversity in housing issues, the plan must indicate that during its preparation, data regarding census tract by race as far back as 1980 were considered. Okay, if that's the case, then in some document someplace - I would call it a general plan "Backgrounding Report" - somebody better make sure that there is a table showing census tracts by race as far back as 1980. A consultant might write 15 pages about the subject. If you are just trying to meet minimum requirements so that you can qualify for some state grant or program, you can just include the chart with a statement to the effect that "... and data regarding census tract by race as far back as 1980 were considered..." That would very likely save you thousands of dollars, and the same process can be followed throughout the preparation of your plan - ultimately saving you tens of thousands of dollars.

Finally, your staff should review the court decisions ("case law") made in relation to the state's general planning statutes. These would rarely comprise more than a dozen pages themselves, and the state chapter of the APA should be very helpful in locating those materials. In most states a compilation of such decisions related to the planning statutes has already been made by the Governor's office, or some other state office responsible for planning. Before beginning the preparation of a city plan, these judicial interpretations should be reviewed to determine to what extent they introduce requirements for a city plan above and beyond what is clearly stated in the statutes.

In summary, your staff needs to collect and become familiar with:
- State Planning Statutes related to municipal planning
- Executive Branch Guidelines, Opinions, or other directives related to municipal planning (including state Attorney General opinions)
- Case law related to municipal planning

OTHER CONSIDERATIONS

To be fully aware of the actual requirements that will need to be met to qualify your general plan for state or federal support, consider who will determine what it means to achieve meet requirements such as "address climate change." It will not be someone from the legislative branch who wrote the legislation, it will be someone from the executive branch, who may not feel much allegiance to the legislation as it was written - and who's primary allegiance will be to their executive hiring authority; who, in turn, is mostly interested in maintaining the broadest base of support for them, or their boss, so that they can prevail in the next election. What this means is that, if you are a local jurisdiction preparing a master plan for your city, you have a lot of latitude in determining what it means to, for example, "address climate change," and if you want to simply say in your plan that your jurisdiction encourages its citizens to purchase fuel efficient automobiles, and that is the way it is addressing climate change, that will often be a sufficient demonstration that your plan has met that requirement.

All of the forgoing presumes a jurisdiction that would like to invest the least amount of time possible in meeting the state requirements for preparing a complete municipal plan. On the other hand, if your jurisdiction wishes to go beyond the minimum requirements, that is a choice you nearly always have, except if your state has specific limitations on what subjects can be addressed by a municipal plan.

ADOPTING THE PLAN

In most states a city plan must go through public hearings at both the city's planning commission and the city council. The public must be given a certain amount of notice prior to each of those hearings, usually 30 days but sometimes even longer. The planning commission makes its recommendation to the council, and the council holds a new hearing. Once adopted by the council, the Plan becomes part of the city's policies, or laws, until it is amended; unless it's adoption is appealed to the courts, in which case the court will determine whether it is a proper plan or not, and whether the required procedures were followed in its adoption.

APPENDICES

TOWN OF CAVE CREEK GENERAL PLAN

ADOPTED JANUARY 4, 1993

SETTLED 1870 · INCORPORATED 1986

TOWN COUNCIL

James Threadgill, Mayor
Mike Patterson, Vice Mayor
Andrew J. (Jack) Bastine
Russ Carlson
Laura Cox
Lester Rechlin
Ellen Sands-Littleton

PLANNING COMMISSION

Roger Lindus, Chairman
Marc Bailes, Vice Chairman
Joan Dodd
Ann Hady
Roger Kull
John Puls
Jo Schnepf

STAFF

Town Manager - Carl Stephani
Town Planner - Jane Bixler
Executive Secretary - Cheryle Witt
Planning Assistant - Bev Peterson

CAVE CREEK GENERAL PLAN

TABLE OF CONTENTS

			PAGE
Chapter	I.	VISION	1
Chapter	II.	PLAN OBJECTIVE, CONTENTS, PURPOSE and INTENT	2
Chapter	III.	LAND USE ELEMENT	4

    A. Goals & Objectives 4
    B. Policies 4
        1. Residential 4
        2. Design 5
        3. Economy 6
    C. Generalized Land Use Map 6
        1. Desert Country - 1 DU/190,000 sq. ft. 7
        2. Desert Rural - 1 DU/70,000 sq. ft. 7
        3. Residential 7
        4. Commercial Core Areas 7
        5. Historic Town Core (HTC) 8
        6. Potential Future Commercial Areas 8
        7. Open Space and Parks 9

Chapter IV. **CIRCULATION ELEMENT** 10
    A. Goals and Objectives 10
    B. Policies 10
    C. Long Range Improvements 11
        1. Carefree Highway 12
        2. North Loop 12
    D. Trails 12

Chapter V. **PUBLIC FACILITIES and SERVICES ELEMENT** 14
    A. Goals and Objectives 14
    B. Policies 14
        1. Public Buildings 14
        2. Community Sewer 14
        3. Public Safety 15
        4. Parks, Recreation, Open Spaces, Schools 15
        5. Resource Conservation 16

GENERAL PLAN LAND USE AND CIRCULATION ELEMENTS MAP 17

CAVE CREEK GENERAL PLAN

CAVE CREEK: A RURAL DESERT FOOTHILLS COMMUNITY

Chapter I. VISION

The Cave Creek area has a long history of settlement by many creative people displaying both a sense of rugged individualism and a community pride. Current residents represent a diverse populace with a wide variety of backgrounds, lifestyles, and values. Some have come here to hike in the solitude of the desert, others for views inspired by the scenic beauty, or to live and grow along with the natural desert habitat, and others still to enjoy the wide open spaces on horseback. All of us, in one way or another, are attracted to this community that has as its greatest resource the natural features of the upper Sonoran desert and surrounding foothills. We realize the value of a lifestyle which maintains a harmony with this desert environment and strives for a balance between individual property rights and those of the community as a whole.

Future inhabitants will come to this region and thus development is inevitable. It is the objective of this plan to insure the integrity of our natural environment while at the same time providing for ample future growth.

Chapter II. PLAN OBJECTIVE, CONTENTS, PURPOSE AND INTENT

This Plan shall serve as a general guide for the Council, Planning Commission, staff and the public regarding development in the Town. It is not intended to be rigid and does not propose inflexible boundaries between use designations or hard lines between land use intensities. It is a guide for achieving projected growth, and presenting the values of today's residents to future residents for their consideration. This document provides general guidance for more detailed decisions. For further resource information with greater detail about planning considerations, refer to the Supplemental General Plan Information Report dated October, 1992.

Consistency of zoning of specific areas or parcels of land with the General Plan shall be evaluated in terms of plan goals, rather than strict conformance to particular Plan policies or map notations.

It is the responsibility of the Town Council to interpret the General Plan in order to resolve any ambiguities or inconsistencies between plan elements, policies or provisions.

The General Plan consists of the following three elements which have been prepared in accordance with the Urban Environment Management Act, Title 9, Ch. 4, Art. 6, A.R.S.:

- Land Use
- Circulation
- Public Facilities and Services

The Plan's goals are intended to be general statements which reflect the community's ideal. Objectives are more specific statements which provide general targets for reaching the identified goals. In turn, these goals and objectives are translated into policies to implement the General Plan.

This Plan emphasizes goals, objectives and policies which are necessary for the development of a low density rural desert foothills community. The goals included in this Plan may not be entirely achievable nor are they considered to be of equal importance; however, they are meant to provide direction.

The Planning Commission, with input from the public, shall monitor, evaluate and recommend revisions to the General Plan annually, with all major revisions to be considered every five (5) years.

For long range planning purposes, this Plan covers an area which extends beyond the current Town limits. Within the study area is the approximately 27 square mile Town of Cave Creek.

Chapter III. LAND USE ELEMENT

A. Goals & Objectives

To preserve and enhance the diverse rural lifestyles, resources and quality of life in the Town compatible with the rights of individual property ownership; while promoting a stewardship responsibility towards the preservation of the native habitat. This will allow for the orderly evolution of the Town.

- Provide for the continuation of the diverse rural life-styles, values and environmental quality by maintaining a rural residential economy and encouraging a modest central business core.

- Encourage small independent businesses which complement the community's quality of life in order to expand the sales tax base.

- Discourage increased density in residential areas.

- Encourage tourism and development in the commercial town core compatible with our unique heritage.

A modest average annual rate of growth necessary to meet the additional population and housing requirements of the Town and the Study Area is desirable as long as the associated development is consistent with the varied lifestyles of the Town's residents.

B. Policies

1. Residential

- Support desert rural low density housing patterns as the planning area's predominant land use.

- Distribute gross densities in desert rural areas no greater than one dwelling unit per 70,000 square feet.

- Limit higher density areas to core areas having community sewer and water service (public or privately owned).

- Density transfers which result in large lot averages rather than small lot clusters could be made where appropriate for individual properties. Application should be made on a case by case basis to support the overall goals and objectives of this Plan while accommodating unique individual property situations.

- Density transfers that would allow lots smaller than ½ of those allowed by the zoning for the area are strongly discouraged.

2. **Design**

- Insure the preservation of the highly sensitive visual/scenic quality of the planning area through the adoption of appropriate guidelines that maintain sight vistas and a faithfulness to the Sonoran Desert and the individual vegetative community affected.

- Encourage development to be designed and built in harmony with the natural character of the land for other than dispersed low density development through the adoption of design ordinances that will assure the proper understanding of nature as a design issue, both as it relates to the specific site and its extended environment.

- Support design guidelines as informational tools for the integration of dispersed low density single-family housing within the natural environment.

- Support creative and sensitive site planning for non-residential development along Cave Creek Road to minimize the negative effects of this area's inherent "strip" orientation; and to reflect the heritage of the area and promote maintenance and restoration of the desert forest scenic corridor.

2. **Economy**

- Support a single service core (Cave Creek Road Business District) as the mixed-use center for goods, services, and local government for the entire planning area.

- Support retail or tourist oriented businesses and professional offices as a means of providing a limited employment base for residents of the Town.

- Support revitalization and rehabilitation efforts of older Town areas that do not provide safe and sanitary conditions.

C. GENERALIZED LAND USE MAP

The Generalized Land Use Map indicates the intended predominant future function, density and characteristic use of land for the different parts of the Town and the study area. The Plan and Map may not reflect the existing zoning of individual parcels, but rather, generalize desired future land uses and density. The boundaries between use and density designations noted on the map are not fixed precisely. Rather, they indicate general areas wherein the goals of the Plan will be pursued through more detailed planning decisions. A one-to-one correspondence between designations on the map and development decisions is not contemplated. It may be appropriate to vary from the map where it is determined that this would as well or better meet overall Plan goals.

The map suggests an overall mix of densities and should not be read as tying individual projects to density designations. To achieve appropriate balance among the goals promoted by the Plan, flexibility in specific decisions is required.

Each project should be evaluated within the context of the area in which it is located and the overall mix of densities that may be possible or appropriate within this area.

1. **Desert Country - maximum 1 DU/190,000 square feet**

   - This is the area that has historically been zoned for 190,000 square foot minimum lot sizes and other large lot sizes with horse privileges.

2. **Desert Rural - maximum 1 DU/70,000 square feet**

   - Mountainous and desert areas that have historically been zoned for one and two acre lot sizes with horse privileges.

   - Ecologically, these are suited to the lowest intensity single-family land uses compatible with view protection.

3. Residential

The areas designated Residential have historically been zoned for ½ acre lots and higher densities in the vicinity of the Town's commercial core areas.

4. Commercial Core Areas

Although environmental factors were considered in the establishment of limits for the Commercial Core areas, locational issues and projected commercial-industrial floor area demands were the overriding factors in the designation of these areas on the generalized land use map. The areas will serve residents and tourists and is intended to reflect the historical context of a Town settled in the 1880's.

Commercial core areas have been located at prime market driven locations only and sized moderately according to the following criteria:

- The Commercial Office/Service Commercial area includes areas along Cave Creek Road from Skyline south to Carriage. That area should be reflective of commercial service or commercial office uses while tourist oriented uses should be concentrated in the HTC.

- The commercial area at Cave Creek Road and Carefree Highway provides a generalized core area which reflects the intensity of the intersection of these two major arterials.

- The commercial core/industrial center at Carefree Highway and 24th Street reflects the long range significance of this area as one which will serve neighborhood needs for the southwest study area and the growing needs of the developing Cave Creek Recreation Area.

5. HTC: Historic Town Core

The Historic Town Core (HTC) is the clearly identifiable area between Scopa Trail and Spur Cross Road. It should contain the neighborhood, office, retail, local government and civic/cultural facilities that will complement a primary tourist/specialty market that is the focus of this core.

The HTC will serve as a community within the community. Regional facilities such as the library, lodging, eating and drinking establishments and entertainment should predominate in this area. There should also be natural open space, passive and low intensity parklands and pedestrian oriented facilities. As such, it should include a variety of housing opportunities including high density multiple family housing and high density single family housing. This housing should allow for a mix of living experiences including the young, area employees and the elderly.

Within the HTC development should be oriented towards low-rise facilities so as to maintain the scale of the historical development of the Town and so as to encourage the development of architectural themes and site amenities that reflect the historical context of the Town.

Guidelines should not attempt to dictate building style but shall encourage buildings which are sensitive to their settings, the neighboring buildings, and the continuity of the desert.

Development in the HTC should encourage and consider incentives for projects. Projects should provide the best possible mix of uses; the most amenities and appropriate infra-structure improvements that will result in the least negative impact on adjacent land uses; and which will address overall preservation of views and native habitat, minimize traffic intrusions and provide building scale and orientation which invites pedestrian use of the development and surrounding areas.

6. Potential Future Commercial Areas

o   Proposed Commercial Areas - The sites for the proposed commercial areas identified on the Generalized Land Use Map more than accommodate projected demand and future growth contingencies for non-residential land uses in the study area.

o   Carefree Highway Corridor - This area is recognized as a zoning impact area that will be aggravated by future growth in traffic counts on Scottsdale Road, Cave Creek Road and Carefree Highway. Projected commercial land area for the coming years does not justify other major cores or strip development along this corridor. Arbitrary designation of commercial use along this core would also necessitate "transitional" land uses with heavy infrastructure costs which will work a severe hardship on the financial capacity of the Town. Therefore, the existing low density residential uses along this corridor should be protected from the adverse impacts of traffic generated by this arterial and pressure for future industrial development. Existing industrial zoning on the South side of Carefree Highway is not considered precedent setting.

o   Sand and Gravel Operation - This land use is incompatible with the adjoining properties. Providing high intensity uses adjoining this nuisance operation would not resolve the area-wide adverse impacts of the operation. The site should eventually be restored to contours suitable for use for low density residential development.

7. OS: Open Space and Parks

The lands within these areas are appropriate for the following uses:

- Riparian and desert wash areas that should be preserved as part of the native habitat.
- Cave Creek Recreation Area.
- Black Mountain Preserve.
- Future active or passive park lands.
- Conservation easements.

While some of these areas are privately owned, they are designated on the plan for open space uses because they indicate the location of floodplains and other special natural areas. While certain preferred uses are indicated for the property, this plan is not intended to deprive any private owner of individual property rights.

Chapter IV. CIRCULATION ELEMENT

A. Goals and Objectives

A system of roads and trails must be established and built that will allow:

- Minimum impact to the native habitat.

- The movement of people between their residences and the Cave Creek Road Business and Civic District.

- Access to all by public safety vehicles.

- Smooth movement of goods and people by aligning alternate routes through Town.

- A road and trail system for the Town based upon the financial objective of construction costs being borne primarily by private land owners and maintenance being the primary responsibility of the Town; with all Town maintained roads being in public ownership.

- A road and trail system which provides circulation for people, vehicles bicycles, and horses to support and enhance the life-styles of Cave Creek; while reinforcing a very low density population pattern.

- Handicapped accessibility for the full use of the Cave Creek Road Business and Civic District.

- Transportation for the handicapped and elderly provided in the Town through community organizations, private providers and other public agencies.

B. Policies

- Require all circulation elements to be on public rights-of-way or along environmental easements dedicated to the public.

- Support multiple use of trails for equestrian, pedestrian and bicycle use.

- Require public access provisions to all public trail segments.

- Support efforts to bring all existing roads and rights-of-ways necessary for public access/circulation under the public domain.

- Utilize improvement districts to improve and expand existing roads and circulation elements.

- Require the construction of an all weather road across Cave Creek Wash in conjunction with development in the north western quarter of the Town.

- Minimize road improvements, where practical, while assuring dust control measures.

- Require improvements at urbanized points along the trails, such as the Cave Creek Road Business and Civic District, to assure adequate areas for bicycle parking and horse hitching and proper paths for allowing movement of pedestrians, bicycles and horses within the district.

- Encourage Town representation on regional transportation and circulation planning committees.

- Require ordinance provisions for developer construction of project related roads and trails and off-site improvements as necessary to properly support the smooth and safe function of the impacted circulation system and to revegetate disturbed areas.

- Encourage private organizations to assist the Town in the development and maintenance of the public trail system.

- Control access partially on Cave Creek Road and Carefree Highway. This means that large scale new developments should be limited to ingress and egress to these highways at section lines, or at ¼ or ½ section lines. Developments on individual lots fronting these highways are encouraged to develop with common driveways serving two or more land uses.

C. **Long Range Improvements**

It is recommended that bike lanes and equestrian/pedestrian trails, and re-vegetation of disturbed areas be included as part of the final improvements for all future roads being considered.

1. Carefree Highway

It is recommended that Carefree Highway be developed as a four-lane section similar to Cave Creek Road with a landscaped median, consistent with the long-range planning of Scottsdale. A wider road would not be compatible with the community desire for low density residential development.

2. Loop Roads

With development to the north, including such lands as the Cahava Ranch property and state lands adjoining the Tonto National Forest, it is recommended that an extension of 24th Street allow for a loop intersection with Schoolhouse Road extended; and provide for access to and from the state lands to the north.

Development between Carefree Highway and New River Road, as well as increased use of the Cave Creek Recreation Area will necessitate the improvement of a southern east/west route of this collector loop. The Town supports the maintenance of an east/west corridor approximating the current location which maintains the integrity of the existing neighborhood.

The acquisition of right-of-way dedications should be a priority.

D. Trails

As part of the overall circulation plan, the General Plan provides for the integration of public trails for equestrian/pedestrian uses and bike lanes into the long range vehicular circulation plan. For the most part, the trails as designated on the accompanying maps include public trails which fall within road right-of-ways for the year 2010 circulation plan. For equestrian/pedestrian trails this means extending trails along one or both sides of the road on a properly graded side slope. For bike lanes this means 5' wide paved shoulders in both directions.

These trails are intended to provide access to the Cave Creek Recreation Area, the Tonto National Forest, the Historic Town Center and to interrelate with other public trails to and from the Cave Creek Area. These trails should be signed as public trails for use by the general public. The accompanying trail maps are intended to provide a conceptual development plan for the long range development of public and private trails in the study area. It is intended that all collector and arterial streets should include public equestrian, pedestrian and bicycle lanes.

- Horseback riding hiking are important elements in Cave Creek lifestyles, and the preservation of historic trails should be encouraged.

- New development is encouraged to maintain the integrity of the historic trails system and to create new public trail corridors.

- Future developments should be encouraged to interrelate to these public trails. Horse trails should be provided along Spur Cross and Schoolhouse Roads.

Chapter V. PUBLIC FACILITIES and SERVICES ELEMENT

A. Goals and Objectives

To provide public facilities and services through a carefully selected mix of public, quasi-public and private providers so as to assure reliable service to the present and future residents of the Town, and which will assure Town control over the actual provision of these services.

B. Policies

1. Public Buildings

o Locate Town offices in the Historic Town Center with ample land area for long term growth and development.

o As the need develops or land becomes available, secure a site for a Public Works Yard.

2. Community Sewer

o Community sewer collection and treatment will be necessary for those areas where higher densities and intensities make on-site sewage absorption a health hazard and threaten to contaminate the ground water.

o Establish the Cave Creek Road Business and Civic District as the number one priority area for community sewer service in the Town.

o Encourage the Town to develop sewer systems for the HTC and future commercial needs.

o Support the dedication of any private sewer system(s) to the Town to assure long-term reliability.

o Support Town consideration of contracting with private operator for management, operation and maintenance of the system.

3. **Public Safety**

   o   Contract for services for the provision of quality and reliable service for police protection.

   o   Consider contracting for fire protection and EMS.

   o   Select locations for facilities for public safety service providers in consultation with the service providers.

4. **Parks, Recreation, and Schools**

Parks may be largely undeveloped with the exception of paths, tables and benches, ramadas or playground equipment. Lighting and other facilities are not required. Linear parks can be developed along Cave Creek Road and natural trail areas to serve neighborhoods. Neighborhood park areas can be encouraged through subdivision development in the future.

   o   Support the development of a low impact community park within the HTC.

   o   Support recreational youth and other community programs offered by other jurisdictions and area organizations, agencies and volunteer groups.

   o   Provide access to the Cave Creek Recreation Area by the Town's circulation system.

   o   Work with School District officials to assure the continuance of a school campus within the Town boundaries and promote recreational opportunities at school facilities.

   o   Open spaces should remain in a natural condition, and affected new developments should enhance them. Open spaces should be interconnected to provide functional links between various parts of the Town and, in the case of washes, be maintained as natural flood control areas. A program for acquiring open space corridors along the washes for trails, either as easements or fee title, should be implemented when financially feasible.

5. Resource Conservation

The Town encourages efforts to conserve water and guarantee its beneficial use and will:

- Consider effects of future development on water resources.

- Develop an effluent reuse system and management policies to guide efficient use of reclaimed water.

- Establish a water management plan to encourage cutting water consumption of underground sources to state mandates.

- Support public and private groundwater recharge efforts.

The Town also encourages:

- Design of energy efficient structures for public and private development and protection of solar access of adjacent facilities.

- Promotion of the use of landscaping which conserves energy and water, shade where effective, and arid plant materials in parks and right-of-ways.

- Promotion of energy efficient development patterns by:

    - Encouraging infilling of vacant areas within developed areas of Town.

    - Minimizing use of heat absorptive surfaces that do not serve an essential function.

    - Planning land use patterns that shorten travel distances for employment and essential services, allowing for alternate modes of transportation and generally conserving energy. Delivery of Town services should be conducted in energy efficient manner.

TOWN OF CAVE CREEK
GENERAL PLAN
SUPPLEMENTAL INFORMATION REPORT

ADOPTED JANUARY 4, 1993

SETTLED 1870 · INCORPORATED 1986

GENERAL PLAN SUPPLEMENTAL INFORMATION REPORT

TABLE OF CONTENTS

			PAGE
I.	Introduction		1
	A.	Description of the Study Area	2
	B.	Projected Growth Through Year 2010	3
	C.	Environment Setting and Scenic Quality	4
	D.	Natural Area Retention	5
	E.	Population Density/Dwelling Units Per Acre	5
II.	Regional Transportation and Circulation		7
	A.	Functional System Characteristics	7
		1. Major Arterial System	7
		2. Collector Street System	8
		3. Local Street System	8
	B.	Roadway Plans and Designs	9
III.	Public Facilities and Services		10
	Elementary Schools		10
	Recreation Areas		10
	Existing Recreation Areas		10
	Future Parklands		11
	Open Space		11
	Public Buildings		11
	Public Works and Public Safety		12
	Solid Waste		12

SUPPLEMENTAL INFORMATION REPORT

I. Introduction

In sections of the Plan, reference is made to other documents which are incorporated in the "Technical Guide, Cave Creek Comprehensive General Plan" and the "Background Report, Cave Creek Comprehensive General Plan". These documents provide greater detail about planning considerations. Documents in the Background Report are illustrative and additional materials developed as references for the General Plan, specific plans, and the development of the Town infrastructure.

This supplemental information is designed to provide additional information regarding the Town's physical and cultural environment.

This Supplemental Information, the Historic Town Core Guidelines, the Technical Guide, and the Background Report are the source materials to be used in interpreting the General Plan. The following documents are part of the Technical Guide: "Current Demographic Profile and Alternative Future Development Scenarios for the Town of Cave Creek", hereinafter referred to as the ASU Report; "Visual Impact Analysis, Town of Cave Creek" ; "Environmental Overview", including soils, hydrology, vegetation, slope, geology and ecological interpretation; "Drainage Study for the Town of Cave Creek"; "Town of Cave Creek Circulation Study"; "Cave Creek Historic Town Core Concept Plan"; and "General Plan Design Guidelines".

The "Background Report, Cave Creek Comprehensive General Plan" contains: description of the Study Area, Socioeconomic Setting, Existing Environment, Soils, Hydrology, Vegetation, Slopes, Scenic Evaluation, Geology, Climate and Air Quality, Ecological Interpretation, Existing and Future Land Use Analysis, Capital Improvement Projects, Bibliography.

Quality of life issues on a community level have most to do with community size, level of governmental service and the overall environmental setting of each resident's dwelling. Today, Cave Creek's "quality of life" offers a small rural community, with minimal governmental services, in a remote setting with a fairly good balance between the human population (and their built environment) and the desert-mountain environment of the study area.

They will be redefined and will evolve as demographic characteristics of the study area's population change, as more development takes place, and as surrounding growth in the greater Metropolitan Phoenix area more directly impacts life in the study area.

A. Description of the Study Area

The study area limit on the east is coincident with the Town's eastern boundary along the Town of Carefree and County lands north of Carefree. To the north the study area extends to the Tonto National Forest. On the west, the study area covers the land between the Town's western boundary and 24th Street extended. The southern boundary of the study area extends one mile south of the Carefree Highway to the east-west alignment of Dove Valley Road.

The study area includes varied topography ranging from gently rolling hills to mountainous area. The 4.5 square mile Maricopa County Cave Creek Recreational Area lies within the Town limits. The study area is predominately contained in a Sonoran desert habitat. The area is in a setting at the upper limits of what the USDA Soil Conservation Service has delineated as the "Central Arizona Basin and Range" bordering the "Arizona and New Mexico Mountains" Major Land Resource Areas (1971).

Settlement, at present, is light (2,925 in the Town limits) with the majority of the population and built environment being east of Cave Creek Wash.

The outlying region of the study area is relatively primitive and undisturbed. The natural environment provides a striking visual setting for the community and is a significant factor to be considered in planning decisions. Although some manmade developments such as power lines, roadcuts and buildings create intrusions in the natural landscape, they do not detract from the spectacular overall visual quality of the area.

These features are presented in the Background Report for the Plan and are, in certain instances, presented in detail in the Technical Guide that is referenced in this General Plan.

Today, Cave Creek's "quality of life" offers a small rural community, with minimal governmental services, in a remote setting with a fairly good balance between the human population (and their built environment) and the desert-mountain environment of the study area.

B. Projected Growth Through Year 2010

PROJECTED GROWTH: YEAR 2010

TOWN LIMITS		
	1990	2010
Population	2430	3599
Dwelling Units	1176	1886

(See ASU Report for detailed projection data.)

Overall, the implementation of this plan will increase the existing study area's residential density from about one dwelling unit per 23.5 acres to about one dwelling unit per 7.5 acres. This density increase will:

- Allow for orderly growth as currently projected in this Plan.
- Allow for the maintenance of the area's environmental integrity.
- Allow adequate vacant developable land area for orderly growth beyond the year 2010.

Based upon analysis of the Background Report and previously referenced source materials, land use categories were developed for designation on the Generalized Land Use Map. In addition to the principal and related land use within each designated land use function, there are four criteria which are of prime importance to these land use categories. They are:

1. Environmental setting and scenic quality.

2. Predominant land use intensity as related to general characteristics of the designated area.

3. Population density/dwelling units (DU) per acre.

4. Concept of natural area retention.

Because of their importance to the plan, these items are being explained on the following pages.

C. Environmental Setting and Scenic Quality

Preliminary background work related to this plan preparation identified the environmental setting and scenic quality of the area as being critical issues to be integrated into the ultimate development of a general plan for the area. Separate reports are referenced in this General Plan which analyze and quantify the environmental and scenic characteristics of the area. Briefly, each respective report addresses the following issues as they relate to the development of land use categories.

The study area lies on the northern edge of the Basin and Range physiographic province in the foothills of Arizona's mountainous region. The New River Mountains and New River Mesa are north of the Study Area. Continental Mountain rises along the eastern boundary. Black Mountain is the south-east boundary and Apache Peak is on the northwest.

In the north and central portions of the Study Area, topography is characterized by numerous low mountains and hills separated by deep valleys. The average height of the mountains is between 3000 and 5000 feet above sea level. The valleys are 2000 to 2200 feet above sea level.

In the southwest corner of the Study Area, the relief opens up into a broad alluvial fan. Here the elevations range between 1780 and 2000 feet above sea level. Specific items evaluated in the designation of land use categories are as follows:

- Soils
- Hydrology
- Vegetation
- Slope
- Geology
- Ecological Interpretation

The visual analysis of the Town of Cave Creek and its surrounding area is composed of several individual studies. It is intended to describe the existing conditions of the area and to show where problem situations may occur. The analysis of the Study Area has been broken down into four categories plus a summary. They are:

- Scenic Quality
- Visual Sensitivity
- Distance Zones
- Visual Classifications

D. **Natural Area Retention**

As reflected in the General Plan's background report, and the "Environmental Overview Report", the Cave Creek Study Area contains natural areas that require special consideration when planning new developments for the future.

Consequently, the concept of "natural area retention per development" has been established as recommended retention of a specified percentage of the total gross area of the planned new development in its natural state. These targets serve as guidelines and also to alert all concerned that there are special issues that recommend themselves to the well thought out integration of natural areas into new development plans. Among them are issues related to:

- o   Minimizing erosion problems.
- o   Maintaining natural drainage ways.
- o   Preserving riparian areas.
- o   Maintaining the flavor of the natural desert environment.
- o   Preserving views and the natural vegetation that provide the backdrop for these views.
- o   Controlling storm water run off.

It is recommended that the concept of natural area retention be applied so as to integrate the retained areas as part of the individual lots within the proposed subdivision/development. This will provide a mechanism for the preservation of these areas and leave them in private ownership without creating arbitrary "islands" of desert that do not relate to actual living experiences.

Population Density/Dwelling Units Per Acre

The "Current Demographic Profile and Alternative Future Development Scenarios for the Town of Cave Creek" (ASU Report) has projected a population of 8,600 persons in the study area by the year 2010. The total number of dwelling units that have been projected as necessary to support this population is 4,050. The results are an average population of 2.12 persons per dwelling unit.

The General Plan reflects this population density in terms of a target range of future dwelling units per acre. This density range provides a quantitative planning guide for evaluating future development plans within the goals, objectives and development policies of the plan. In the purest form, application of the recommended density for each designated land use area would result distribution of dwelling units throughout in a relatively uniform an area at total buildout.

The density ranges of each land use category have been proposed with an understanding of:

- The rights maintained on individual platted lots to be developed according to the maximum density of the legally adopted zoning ordinance that governs them.

- The right of land owners to prepare land use plans and plats and resultant densities according to the legally adopted zoning ordinance that governs them.

Terrain conditions, individual site configurations, circulation needs, existing platted lots, existing zoning standards, existing development patterns and market conditions, among other considerations, will likely result in a mix of dwelling unit types and densities - both higher and lower - within the target range for the broad areas that typically make up a land use category.

II. Regional Transportation and Circulation

Town participation in regional planning studies for transportation systems and networks will be necessary to advocate plans that are in the best interest of the Town's life-style objectives.

All circulation maps are part of the Circulation Element. They include:

- Functional Classifications
- Major Street Design Criteria
- Equestrian and Pedestrian Trails
- Bicycle Lanes

In a smaller urban area, such as Cave Creek, there are a limited number and extent of important streets and highway systems that can be classified as "major arterials". Major arterials for the year 2010 in the Cave Creek study area will include two highways.

A. Functional System Characteristics

The primary functional street categories in the Cave Creek study area are as follows:

- Major Arterials
- Minor Arterials
- Collector Streets
- Local Streets

1. Major Arterial System

- Carefree Highway
- Cave Creek Road

A major arterial is intended to provide service to: major centers of activity, traffic volume corridors, and the longest trip desires. It should carry a high proportion of the study area travel on a minimum of mileage and will carry the major portion of trips entering the study area, as well as the majority of through movement bypassing the study area.

In addition, these arterials should serve significant intra-area travel between Cave Creek and Central Phoenix and/or major suburban centers. The principal arterial system will potentially carry important intra-urban bus routes and should be designed with designated bike lanes and pedestrian/equestrian trails.

Carefree Highway - Carefree Highway serves as a major east/west link between Scottsdale Road on the east and I-17 on the west. Furthermore, Carefree Highway will provide a key link between major outlying recreational areas and urban population centers. On the west is Lake Pleasant. On the east is Bartlett Lake and other remote recreational areas.

Cave Creek Road south of Carefree Highway - Cave Creek Road, south of Carefree Highway provides an important link between the Cave Creek study area and the major centers of activity in Metropolitan Phoenix. It will also provide a link to the planned outer loop at Beardsley Road.

2. **Collector Street System**

Northern Loop - The minor arterials will include connections to a long range proposal for a rural collector loop. On the north, this loop is proposed to extend east/west between School House Road extended and Twenty-Fourth Street extended. On the south, this loop will be Rodeo Road/New River Road running east/west between Twenty-Fourth Street and Cave Creek Road.

School House Road Extended - School House Road will collect and distribute traffic to and from residential neighborhoods from Cave Creek Road to the Tonto Forest.

The collector street system for Cave Creek will provide both land access service and traffic circulation within residential neighborhoods. It differs from the arterial system in that facilities on the collector system will penetrate residential neighborhoods, and distribute trips from the arterials through the area to their ultimate destination. Conversely, these collector streets will also collect traffic from local streets in residential neighborhoods and channel it into the arterial system.

Although there are existing streets within the Cave Creek study area that may loosely be considered collector streets, the low density nature of the area and the limited service area of these roads have precluded the designation of additional collector streets in the study area at this time.

3. **Local Street System**

The local streets primarily provide direct access to abutting land and access to the higher order of street systems. it offers the lowest level of mobility and usually contains no bus routes.

B. Roadway Plans and Designs

There are three levels of plans presented for roads and bike lanes.

- Existing - Current street, with or without planned improvements.
- Planned - In design, construction likely to follow.
- Long Range - A conceptual route which may be beyond the time frame of this plan.

Tentative plans by the City of Phoenix include the construction of paved bike lanes and appropriate grading for equestrian/pedestrian trails in the right-of-way for that portion of Cave Creek Road south of Carefree Highway.

The appearance of the study area's major streets is important to the Town and to values of adjoining properties. Therefore, it is recommended that the final year 2010 development of these roads fall within a parkway or scenic corridor.

Parkways - A facility with a center median that is landscaped with native vegetation. Also non-intrusive native shrubs should be maintained on the outer limits of the right-of-way.

Scenic Corridor - Any street type that is designated to create an atmosphere of a desert-like drive. The scenic corridor differs from the parkway in that standards are developed with adjoining private properties for the preservation of native vegetation and the protection of views to background areas.

III. Public Facilities and Services

At present, the Town provides few public facilities and services directly. The "Background Report" will provide ideas and insights into the provision of specific infrastructure facilities and services, particularly sewer and water.

There are specific public facility and service considerations that should be discussed in further detail. They include the continuance of an elementary school in the Town, the provision of parks and recreational facilities in the Town, and future public building needs.

Elementary Schools

Cave Creek has had a public school in the area for nearly 100 years. The presence of a public school provides an important community focal point for the Town. It serves as a functional element of a total community for the residents of the area. Furthermore, it provides a visual confirmation to tourists and those on day trips to the area that the Town is a total community which coincidentally provides attractions and facilities for nonresidents.

Recreation Areas

The Town of Cave Creek does not currently provide for park lands and recreation sites. Ample opportunity exists for the Town to meet these needs through existing facilities and the development of new and/or replacement sites as needed during the time frame of the General Plan.

Existing Recreation Areas

1. Cave Creek Elementary School playground and grass lot provides for active recreation and sports during after school hours. This school may be relocated within 4-7 years, creating the need for replacement of a central playground/park area by the Town.

2. Active sport fields at Black Mountain School and Cactus Shadows School provide for adult and child team sports in the community when scheduled after school use hours. These facilities may become less available for community use as school activities increase.

3. Cave Creek Recreation Area (Maricopa County Parks & Recreation) is oriented toward a nature study area, with existing equestrian trails and planned campgrounds.

4. Desert Foothills Community Association (DFCA) holds a lease on approximately 10 acres at the southwest corner of the Cave Creek Recreation Area. Improvements to date include a well and rodeo arena and grounds (Memorial Arena Grounds).

5. The Pageant Grounds is a privately owned open space used annually by the Cave Creek Improvement Association for the Christmas Pageant. This area is currently in escrow (5/88). It is hoped that an arrangement will be reached with the future property owners for continued use of this space for the pageant and possible use as a passive park at other times of the year.

Future Parklands

1. County-owned land adjacent to the rodeo grounds (within Town limits).

2. The Maricopa County landfill, when it is reclaimed.

The crest and much of the north face of Black Mountain was purchased by residents of Cave Creek in the early 1960's from the Bureau of Land Management (BLM.) This land was turned over to the Maricopa County Parks and Recreation authority on the stipulation that it remain as a preserve in its natural state.

Open Space

As identified on the Land Use Map, Open Space delineation falls within three principal land form areas.

In turn, each of these open space land forms is a principal means of preservation of significant natural resource areas and wildlife habitat.

Public Buildings

As the Town matures and opportunities arise, the Town and public agencies will inevitably need to add public buildings and facilities. Among them will be Town offices, cultural facilities and a public works yard.

At present there is a modern library in the Town and a modern museum, both operated by nonprofit organizations. The museum is located on the northwest corner of Skyline Drive and Basin Road. The library is just north of Cave Creek Elementary School on School House Road. Additional cultural/community facilities may be possible within the 20 year timeframe of this General Plan.

Public Works and Public Safety

Future public works space and facilities needs will primarily be related to the provision of a field office and storage yard for future street and traffic maintenance operations. However, should the Town provide community sewer and water services, these functions and related equipment could be combined at one location.

At the present time police and fire protection and emergency medical services are provided on a contract basis. As such, the Town has not had to provide plant facilities for these operations.

This will continue with police protection, as the Sheriff's Department will soon be providing a new substation off of New River Road/Rodeo Drive on County parkland.

Should the Town contract directly with the provider of fire protection and emergency medical service (rather than the current system of individual contracts between the provider and property owner), the Town may be required to provide the physical plant for these services.

Solid Waste

Solid waste collection will remain a property owner's responsibility, while the Town will work with the County to assure a safe and sanitary solid waste disposal site.

If you enjoyed this book, please enter your positive comments about it in a review on www.amazon.com or another internet book review web site. You may also enjoy the following other books written by Carl and Marilyn:

ON BECOMING A CITY MANAGER
A Chronicle of Intrigue and Deception

THE KINDNESS OF RANDOM STRANGERS
Hitchhiking San Diego to Panama 1961

ZONING 101
A Practical Introduction

You can contact the authors at: carl@carlstephani.com

CPSIA information can be obtained
at www.ICGtesting.com
Printed in the USA
BVHW030004240119
538508BV00014B/21/P